BARCELONA
ARCHITECTURE & DESIGN

daab

Seit den Neunzigerjahren haben in Barcelona große ästhetische Veränderungen stattgefunden. Anlässlich der Olympischen Spiele im Jahr 1992 wurden zahlreiche architektonische Eingriffe vorgenommen, die die Hauptstadt des Modernismus veränderten. Wo vorher die Werke Gaudís vorherrschten, fanden jetzt zahlreiche urbanistische Umgestaltungen statt, und es entstanden Gebäude von bekannten spanischen und auch ausländischen Architekten. Besonders zu erwähnen sind dabei der Palau Sant Jordi von Isozaki, die Telekommunikationstürme von Foster und Calatrava und der Fisch von Gehry. Diese Bauwerke teilen sich nun die Stadt mit der Pedrera und der Sagrada Familia und machen sie im weltweiten Kontext wettbewerbsfähig. Barcelona hebt sich auch weiterhin von anderen Städten ab. Das Kulturforum im Jahr 2004 stellte einen weiteren Impuls für die städtebaulichen Veränderungen in der Stadt dar. Für dieses kulturelle Ereignis entdeckte man einen Teil der Stadt neu, der in Vergessenheit geraten war, die Küstenzone am Fluss Besòs. In dieser Zone und in der anliegenden Verlängerung der Allee Diagonal bis zum Meer stand ausreichend Baugelände zur Verfügung, um die notwendigen Gebäude für diese kulturelle Veranstaltung zu errichten. Anlässlich des Forums wurden erneut bekannte Architekten damit beauftragt, ein neues Barcelona zu schaffen. Eine Stadt, die unaufhörlich auf Innovation und Design setzt, ohne ihre reiche architektonische Vergangenheit zu vergessen. Die Stadt Barcelona ist im Laufe der Zeit zu einem Modell für die Kunst geworden, ein kosmopolitisches Vorbild, das anderen Städten als Inspiration dient. Das beweisen sowohl die architektonische Gestaltung der Gebäude als auch die Raumausstattungen und das Innendesign. In beiden Sektoren arbeiten internationale Architektur- und Designstudios häufig mit lokalen Architekten zusammen, eine Zusammenarbeit, aus der sich unterschiedliche und ergänzende Visionen ergeben.

Since the 90's Barcelona has been undergoing a complete makeover in terms of esthetics. The 1992 Olympic Games also brought an infinite number of constructions that transformed the capital of Modernism. Thus, the predominance of works by Gaudi gave way to the proliferation of city-planning changes and buildings designed by the biggest foreign and domestic names in architecture. Works like Isozaki's Palau Sant Jordi, communication towers by Foster and Calatrava and Gehry's fish suddenly coexisted with la Pedrera and Sagrada Familia. The city got ready to compete and stand-out at a world-wide level. Another great architectural and city planning opportunity was provided by the 2004 Forum of Cultures. Thanks to this event, a part of the city which had been neglected was rediscovered: the coastline area beside the Besòs River. This area, together with the prolongation of Diagonal Avenue down towards the sea, provided enough land to construct the buildings that would be necessary to host such an event. With the Forum, the city once again turned to the most renowned architecture studios and handed them the task of creating a new Barcelona. A city that could keep advancing with its insatiable appetite for design and innovation, yet without turning its back on its rich architectural past. Little by little, it's been transformed into an artistic reference, a model that other cities may imitate due to its cosmopolitan nature. This is reflected in its constructions as much as it is their interior designs, fields where we can see increasingly closer collaborations between international studios and local architectures, who by working together offer different, but complementary, visions.

Desde la década de los 90 Barcelona ha experimentado un gran cambio en el ámbito estético. La celebración de los Juegos Olímpicos en 1992 trajo consigo un sinfín de intervenciones que transformaron la capital del Modernismo. Así, la preponderancia de las obras gaudinianas dejó paso a la proliferación de cambios urbanísticos y edificios diseñados por grandes figuras de la arquitectura, extranjeras y nacionales. Obras como el Palau Sant Jordi de Isozaki, la torre de comunicaciones de Foster y la de Calatrava o el pez de Gehry convivían con la Pedrera y la Sagrada Familia; la ciudad se equipó para competir y destacar en el contexto mundial. Otro de los empujes en el orden arquitectónico y urbanístico fue la celebración del Fórum de las Culturas en el 2004. Gracias a este evento se redescubrió una parte de la ciudad que había quedado olvidada: el sector litoral del río Besòs. Esta zona, junto con la prolongación de la avenida Diagonal hasta su encuentro con el mar, proporcionó suficientes terrenos para ubicar los equipamientos necesarios y albergar dicho acontecimiento. Con motivo de este Fórum se recurrió una vez más a renombrados despachos de arquitectura para encargarles la misión de crear una nueva Barcelona. Una ciudad que pudiera seguir avanzando en su imparable apuesta por el diseño y la innovación sin dar la espalda a su histórica riqueza arquitectónica. Poco a poco ha ido transformándose en un referente artístico, un modelo a imitar por otras ciudades debido a su personalidad cosmopolita. Ésta se refleja tanto en sus construcciones como en el diseño de interiores, campos en los que cada vez son más comunes las colaboraciones entre despachos internacionales y arquitectos locales, cuyo trabajo conjunto aporta visiones distintas y complementarias.

Depuis les années 90 Barcelone a connu des changements importants sur le plan esthétique. La célébration des Jeux Olympiques en 1992 a entraîné toute une série d'interventions qui ont profondément modifié le visage de la capitale du Modernisme. Ainsi, un nombre important de modifications urbanistiques et de bâtiments conçus par des grands noms de l'architecture, tant étrangers que nationaux, sont venus occupé la place réservée jusqu'alors aux oeuvres de Gaudi. Des bâtiments comme le Palau Sant Jordi de Isozaki, les tours des télécommunications de Foster et de Calatrava ou encore le poisson de Gehry ont cohabité avec la Pedrera et la Sagrada Familia. La ville s'est transformée pour se faire une place au niveau mondial. La célébration du Forum des Cultures en 2004 a constitué un nouvel élan sur le plan architectural et urbanistique. Grâce à cet événement, la partie littorale du fleuve Besos, oubliée jusqu'alors, a été redécouverte. Cette zone ainsi que le prolongement de l'avenue Diagonal jusqu'à la mer ont fourni assez de terrains pour y implanter les équipements nécessaires et accueillir cet événement majeur. Le Forum a été l'occasion de faire appel à des cabinets d'architectes de renommée internationale chargés de créer une nouvelle Barcelone. Une ville en mesure de poursuivre sur la voie du design et de l'innovation sans tourner le dos à sa richesse architecturale héritée du passé. Peu à peu, Barcelone s'est imposée comme une référence artistique, un modèle à suivre fondé sur son caractère cosmopolite. Celui-ci se reflète tant dans les constructions que dans les designs d'intérieurs. Des domaines dans lesquels les collaborations entre des cabinets internationaux et des architectes locaux sont de plus en plus courantes. Il en résulte des visions différentes et complémentaires à la fois.

A partire dagli anni Novanta, Barcellona ha sperimentato un grande cambiamento di ambito estetico. La celebrazione dei Giochi Olimpici del 1992 ha portato con sé un'infinità di interventi che hanno trasformato la capitale del Modernismo. Così, la preponderanza delle opere di Gaudí ha ceduto il passo al proliferare di trasformazioni urbanistiche e di edifici disegnati da grandi figure dell'architettura, straniere e anche nazionali. Opere come il Palau Sant Jordi di Isozaki, la torre delle telecomunicazioni di Foster e quella di Calatrava o il pesce di Gehry convivevano con la Pedrera e con la Sagrada Familia; la città si è adeguata per competere e farsi notare nel contesto mondiale. Un'altra spinta a livello architettonico e urbanistico è stata la celebrazione del Forum delle Culture del 2004. Grazie a questo evento è stata riscoperta una parte della città che era stata dimenticata: il settore litorale del fiume Besòs. La zona, assieme al prolungamento dell'arteria urbana della Diagonal fino al mare, ha offerto una superficie sufficiente per ubicare le attrezzature necessarie e ospitare l'avvenimento. In occasione del Forum, i progetti sono stati assegnati ancora una volta a famosi studi di architettura che hanno ricevuto l'incarico di creare una nuova Barcellona. Una città che potesse continuare ad avanzare nella sua inarrestabile scommessa sul design e sull'innovazione senza voltare le spalle alla sua storica ricchezza architettonica. Poco a poco è diventato un punto di riferimento artistico, un modello da imitare per le altre città grazie alla sua personalità cosmopolita, che si riflette sia nella sua architettura, sia nel design d'interni, settori in cui sono sempre più comuni le collaborazioni tra studi internazionali e architetti locali, il cui lavoro congiunto apporta visioni distinte e complementari.

ADD+Arquitectura/Xavier Claramunt
Hotel Chic & Basic Born | 2006
Princesa 50, 08001

Dieses einzigartige Hotel liegt in dem Modeviertel der Stadt, Born, wo sich das historische Erbe mit neuen kulturellen und gastrono-mischen Vorschlägen vermischt. Die Besonderheit des Chic & Basic liegt darin, dass sich jeder Kunde seinen Raum nach Maß entwer-fen kann. Das Hotel ist wie eine weiße Leinwand, für die man sich die Farbe des Lichts mithilfe von Leds und Glasfaser auswählen kann, ebenso wie die Musik. In der Dekoration werden zeitgenössische Möbel mit barocken Stücken kombiniert und Leder und Samt mit technologischen Materialien, wodurch dieser sehr „schicke" Stil entsteht.

This unique hotel is located in the Born, the city's fashionable neighborhood, where historical inheritance blends with innovating cul-tural and gastronomical offers. What stands out about Chic & Basic is that each client can design the space to their liking. The hotel is like a white canvas where you can choose the color of light, thanks to the LED and optic fibers, as well as the music. Its décor blends contemporary and Baroque furniture, or skins and velvet with technological materials, giving it a very chic style.

Este singular hotel se encuentra en el Born, el barrio de moda de la ciudad, donde la herencia histórica se mezcla con novedosas pro-puestas culturales y gastronómicas. La particularidad del Chic & Basic estriba en que cada cliente puede diseñar el espacio a su medi-da. El hotel es como un lienzo en blanco donde se puede escoger el color de la luz, gracias a los LED y la fibra óptica, así como la música. Su decoración mezcla mobiliario contemporáneo y barroco o pieles y terciopelos con materiales tecnológicos, lo que le otor-ga un estilo muy chic.

Cet hôtel si singulier se trouve dans le Born, le quartier à la mode de la ville, où l'héritage historique se mêle aux propositions cultu-relles et gastronomiques modernes. La particularité de Chic & Basic réside dans la liberté laissée à chaque client d'agencer l'espace à sa guise. Grâce aux LED et à la fibre optique, l'hôtel est comme une toile blanche pour laquelle on peut choisir la couleur de la lumière mais aussi la musique. Sa décoration réunit le mobilier contemporain et baroque, le cuir et les velours avec des matériaux technolo-giques, ce qui donne un cachet très chic à ce lieu.

Questo singolare hotel si trova nel Born, il quartiere di moda della città, in cui l'eredità storica si mescola a innovative proposte cultu-rali e gastronomiche. La particolarità dello Chic & Basic sta nel fatto che ogni cliente può disegnare il proprio spazio su misura. L'ho-tel è come una tela bianca in cui si può scegliere il colore della luce, grazie ai LED e alla fibra ottica, così come la musica. La decora-zione fonde arredi contemporanei e barocchi o pelli e velluti con materiali tecnologici, assumendo uno stile assai chic.

Chic&basic is different. It's new. It's a concept. It's simple, it's smart, it's surprising. It's open-minded, it's cool. It's fresh. Ideas. It's naughty. Is it possible? Yes, it is. It's contemporary. It's comfortable. It's a nightlife guide. It's easy to check in, it's easy to check out. It's just easy. It's fusion. It's cross-culture. It's Spanish, it's English, it's French, it's bla, bla, bla. It's like... It's Chic, it's Basic, that's what it is.

chic&basic

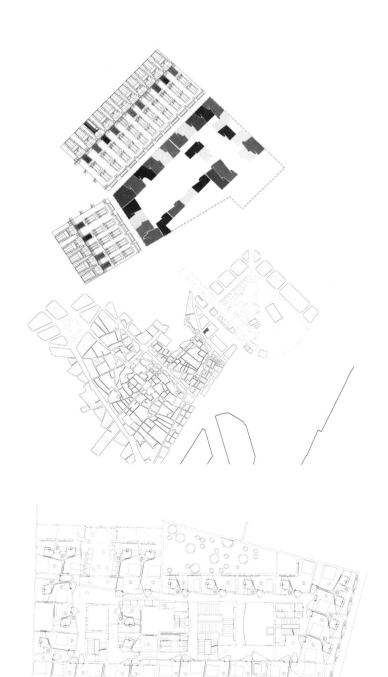

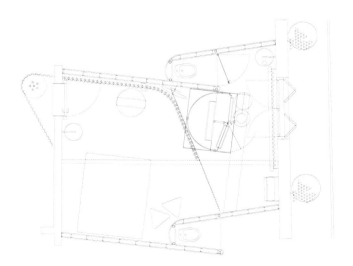

Ateliers Jean Nouvel/Jean Nouvel, b720 Arquitectos/Fermín Vázquez
Agbar Tower | 2005
Avinguda Diagonal 211, 08018

Das Hochhaus Agbar ist heute eines der Wahrzeichen der Stadt. Seine zylindrische, ovale Form, die einer Wasserfontäne nachempfunden ist und somit die Aktivität des in diesem Gebäude untergebrachten Wasserwerks von Barcelona (Agbar) symbolisiert, entspricht nicht der eines konventionellen Wolkenkratzers. Das Gebäude vereint zwei gegensätzliche Konzepte, die Leichtigkeit des Glases, das die Fassade verkleidet, und die Masse des Zements in seiner Struktur. Besonders auffallend ist die nächtliche Beleuchtung, die mit 4000 Elementen erzeugt wird.

Today the Agbar Tower stands as one of the city's greatest emblems. Its shape, a skyscraper that strays from the usual concept with its ovoidal cylindrical shape, designed to emulate a water spout, so as to reinforce its identity as central offices for Aguas de Barcelona (Agbar). The building unites two opposing concepts: on one side, the lightness of the glass that covers the façade and, on the other, the forcefulness of its concrete structure. One of the tower's most characteristic elements is its nighttime lighting, which uses over 4,000 lighting mechanisms.

A día de hoy, la Torre Agbar se ha convertido en uno de los emblemas de la ciudad. Su figura, un rascacielos que escapa al concepto habitual gracias a su forma de cilindro ovoidal, emula un surtidor de agua, lo que refuerza su identidad como sede del grupo Aguas de Barcelona (Agbar). El edificio aúna dos conceptos opuestos: por un lado, la ligereza del vidrio que recubre la fachada y, por otro, la contundencia del hormigón de su estructura. Uno de los elementos más característicos de la torre es su iluminación nocturna, que consiguen más de 4.000 dispositivos luminosos.

La Tour Agbar est devenue l'un des symboles de la ville. Si elle ressemble à un gratte-ciel, elle s'en distingue par sa forme cylindrique ovoïde et sa silhouette rappelant un jet d'eau renforce son identité comme siège du groupe Aguas de Barcelona (Agbar). Le bâtiment réunit deux concepts opposés : la légèreté du verre recouvrant la façade et la puissance du béton de sa structure. L'un des éléments les plus caractéristiques de la tour est son éclairage nocturne composé de 4 000 dispositifs lumineux.

La Torre Agbar è diventata ormai uno degli emblemi della città. La sua figura, che rifugge il concetto abituale di grattacielo grazie alla forma cilindrica ovoidale, ricalca quella di uno zampillo d'acqua, rafforzando la propria identità come sede del gruppo Aguas de Barcelona (Agbar). L'edificio affianca due concetti opposti: da una parte, la leggerezza del vetro che riveste la facciata e, dall'altra, la consistenza del calcestruzzo della struttura. Uno degli elementi più caratteristici della torre è l'illuminazione notturna, costituita da più di 4.000 dispositivi luminosi.

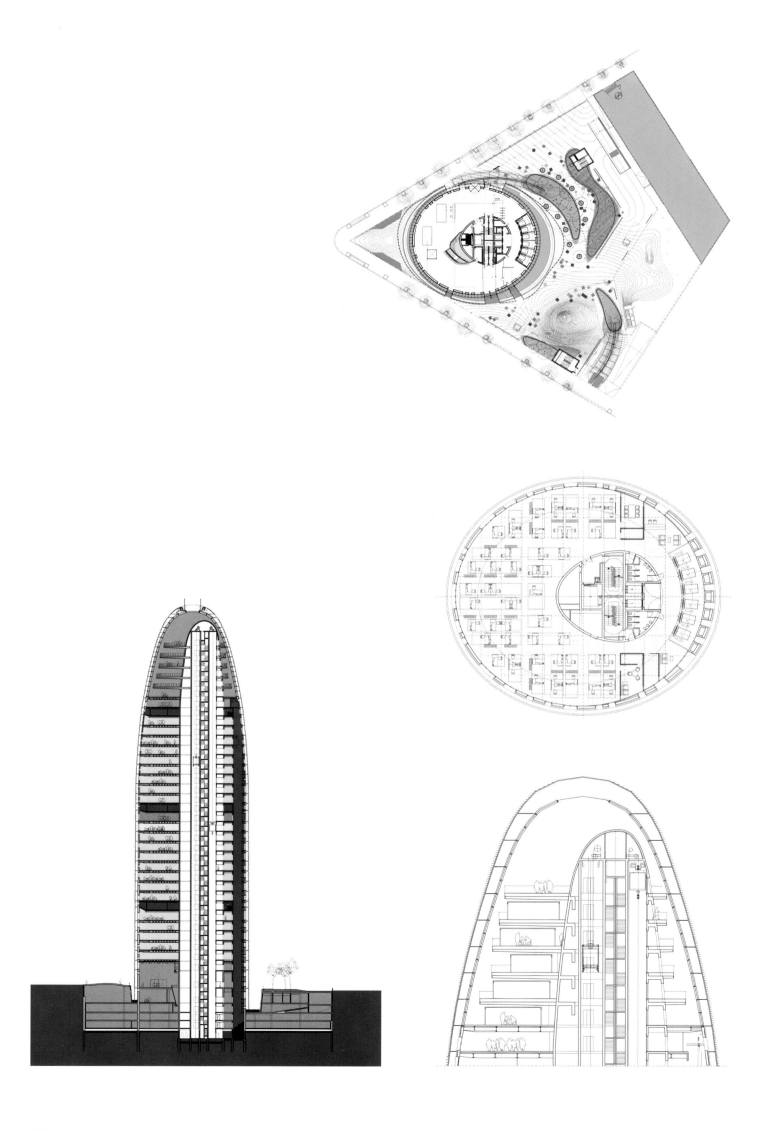

b720 Arquitectos

Indra Offices | 2006

Tànger 110-120, 08018

Über einer dreistöckigen, sockelartigen, massiven und kompakten Struktur erhebt sich eine hohe, schlanke Form mit rhomboidem Grundriss. Da es sich um ein Firmengebäude mit Büroräumen handelt, entwarf man weite, transparente Stockwerke, die jedoch je nach den zukünftigen Notwendigkeiten unterteilt werden können. Die Originalfassade wurde mit einem Metallgewebe aus Edelstahl bekleidet, das mit in das Gewebe gepressten Kugeln bedruckt ist.

Over a more solid and compact three-floor plinth-like structure they've constructed the highest piece, which flaunts its slenderness over a rhomboidal base. Since this is a corporate office building they've designed spacious floors, although projected so they can be divided in different units depending on future needs. The original façade has been covered by a stainless steel metal with spherical patterns inlayed into the material.

Sobre una estructura de tres plantas a modo de zócalo, más maciza y compacta, se alza la pieza más alta que luce su esbeltez sobre una planta romboidal. Al tratarse de un edificio corporativo de oficinas se han diseñado amplias plantas diáfanas, aunque proyectadas para poder dividirse en diferentes unidades según las necesidades futuras. La original fachada está revestida por un tejido metálico de acero inoxidable con estampados en forma de esfera realizados mediante la embutición del tejido.

Sur une structure massive et compacte de trois étages en guise de socle, s'élance la partie la plus élevée sur une base en losange. S'agissant d'un bâtiment abritant les bureaux dune entreprise, il est constitué d'étages amples et lumineux, avec toutefois la possibilité de les diviser en plusieurs unités selon les besoins à venir. La façade originale est recouverte d'une toile métallique en acier inoxydable avec des motifs en forme de sphère réalisés par compression.

Al di sopra di una struttura di tre livelli massiccia e compatta, a mo' di piedistallo, si innalza il volume più alto che esibisce il suo profilo snello a pianta romboidale. Trattandosi di un edificio corporativo per uffici, la costruzione presenta superfici ampie e diafane, anche se sono state progettate in modo da poter essere divise in diverse unità a seconda delle future esigenze. L'originale involucro è rivestito da un tessuto metallico di acciaio inossidabile, con disegni sferici ottenuti attraverso l'imbottitura del tessuto.

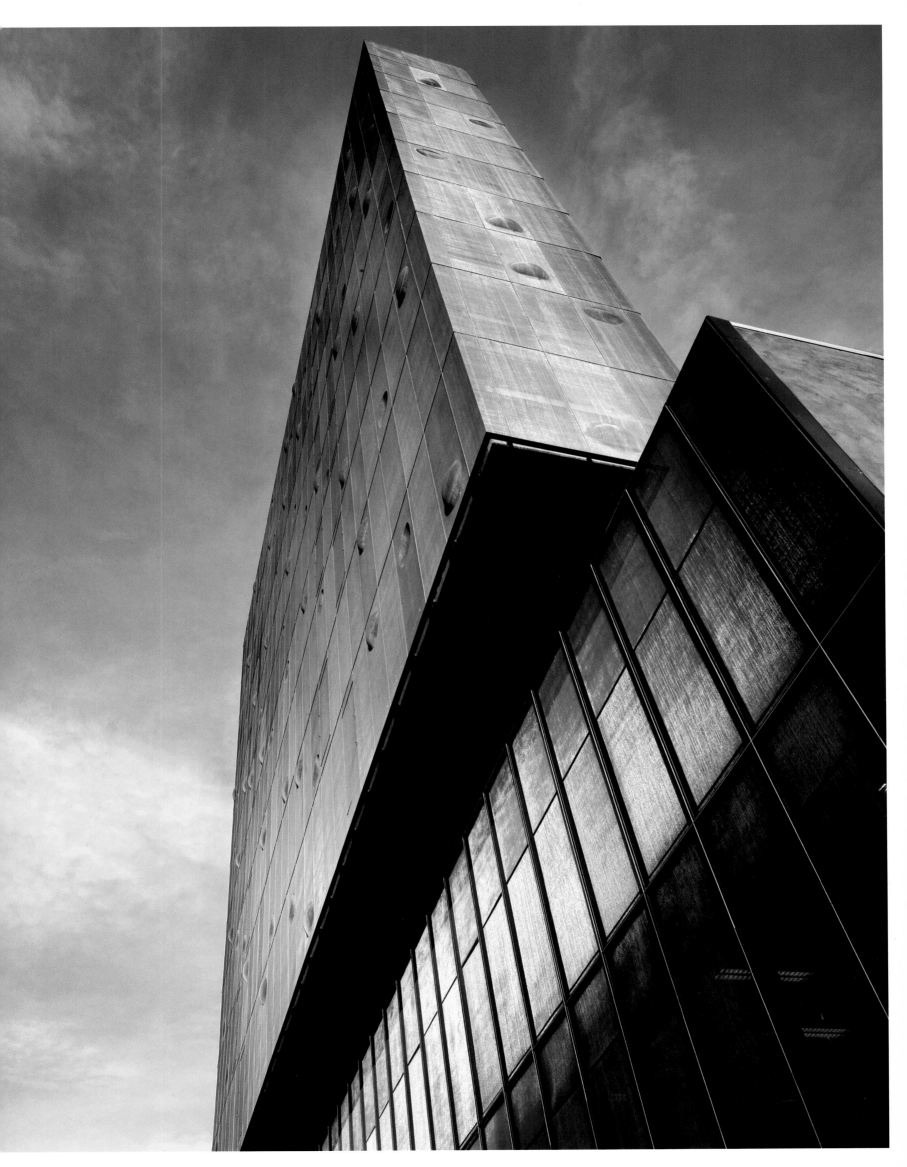

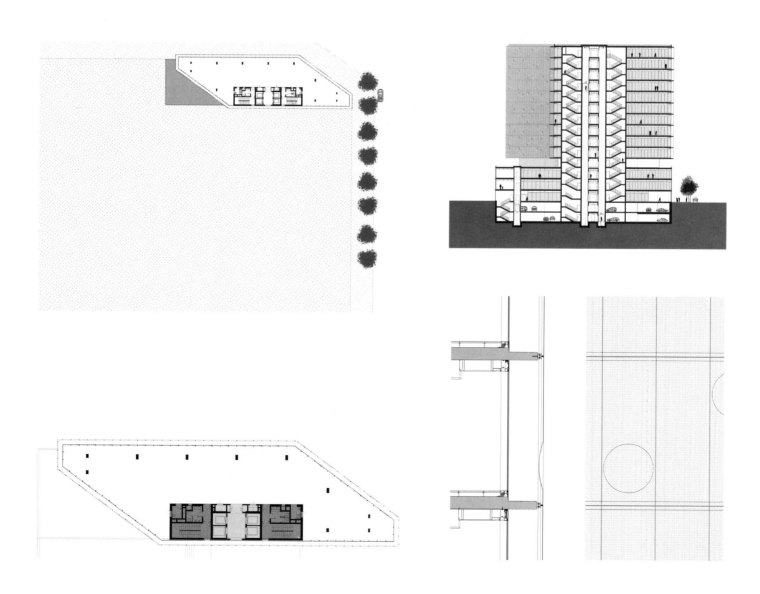

BAAS/Jordi Badia
Refurbishment of a Commercial Space into an Office | 2006
Garcilaso 11-15, 08027

Die auffallende Hauptfassade wurde wie ein großer Holzrahmen aus Kiefer gestaltet, der die Aktivitäten im Inneren umrahmt und für die optische Beleuchtung des Lokals sorgt. Die große Glasfläche am Eingang macht es möglich, dass man von beiden Ebenen im Inneren aus, also vom Erdgeschoss und von der Mansarde, einen Blick nach draußen hat. Die vertikalen Holzlamellen bedecken die ganze Höhe des Lokals und verbergen die privaten Räume, während die übrigen, für die Arbeit bestimmten Räume mit großen, aufgeklebten, fotographischen Drucken auf Vinyl dekoriert sind.

The spectacular main facade was conceived as a large pine wood frame for the activity that goes on inside, while providing the space with optic lighting. The large entrance window allows for the two interior levels, the ground floor and the attic are practically the same size and offer views outside. Vertical wooden slats cover the entire height of the space and conceal private areas, while the rest is decorated with large adhesive vinyl photographic prints and is to be used as work areas.

La espectacular fachada principal ha sido concebida como un gran marco de madera de pino que encuadra la actividad interior y proporciona la iluminación óptica del local. El gran cristal de la entrada permite que los dos niveles del interior, la planta baja y un altillo de prácticamente las mismas dimensiones, tengan vistas al exterior. Las lamas de madera verticales cubren toda la altura del local y esconden los espacios privados, mientras que el resto, decorado con grandes vinilos adhesivos con fotografía impresa, están destinados a los espacios de trabajo.

La spectaculaire façade principale a été conçue comme un grand cadre en bois de pin englobant l'activité intérieure et offrant un éclairage optimal pour le lieu. La grande vitre de l'entrée permet une vue sur l'extérieur depuis les deux niveaux intérieurs, le rez-de-chaussée et la mezzanine de dimensions égales. Les lames de bois verticales recouvrent toute la hauteur du lieu et occultent les espaces privatifs, alors que le reste, décoré de grands vinyles adhésifs avec des photographies imprimées, est destiné aux espaces de travail.

La spettacolare facciata principale è stata concepita come una grande cornice in legno di pino che inquadra le attività all'interno e garantisce l'illuminazione ottica del locale. La grande vetrata dell'ingresso assicura ai due livelli interni, il piano terra e un mezzanino praticamente delle stesse dimensioni, le viste verso l'esterno. Traverse di legno verticali poste a tutta altezza nel locale nascondono gli spazi privati, mentre il resto, decorato con grandi vinili adesivi stampati con fotografie, è destinato alle aree di lavoro.

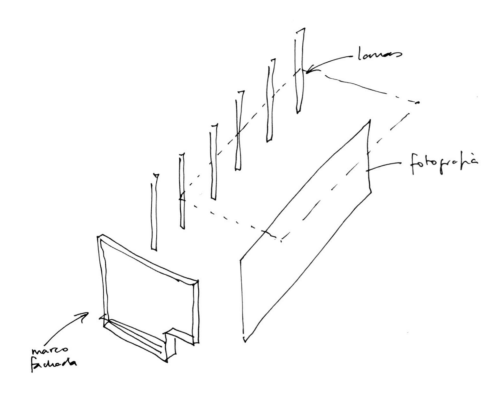

lamas

fotografía

marco fachada

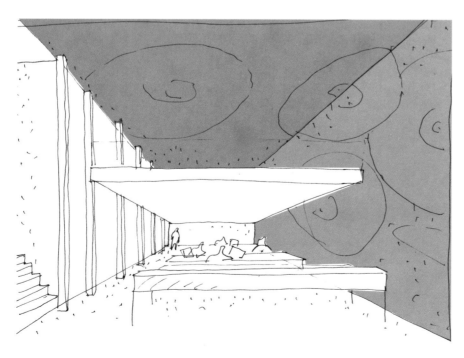

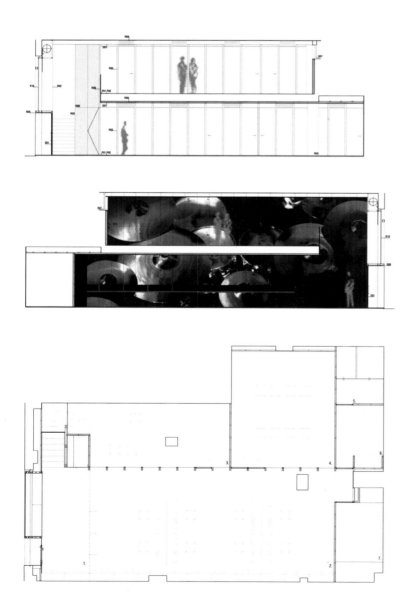

Brullet-Pineda Arquitectes

Barcelona Biomedical Research Park | 2006
Doctor Aiguader 88, 08003

Dieses Gebäude zeichnet sich durch seine auffallende Form aus. Es handelt sich um einen abgestumpften Kegel mit elliptischen Grundriss und einer Größe von 117 x 74 Metern, mit abgeschrägter Kante und Holzverkleidung. Diese Struktur dient als zentraler Raum in Form eines Platzes, der auf der niedrigeren, sich zum Meer hin neigenden Seite des Gebäudes offen ist. Zum zentralen Innenhof weisen zusätzliche Kreisformen, in denen die Diensträume, Büros und Labore des biomedischen Forschungsparks untergebracht sind. Das Zentrum wird als eines der wichtigsten in Südeuropa betrachtet.

The shape of this building is one of its most attractive characteristics. It's a chopped cone with an elliptic base measuring 384 x 243 feet, cut with bevel edges and covered with wood. This structure has a central space shaped as a plaza that is open on the lowest side of the building, which leans towards the sea. Near the central patio we can see some auxiliary areas, behind which we can find the equipment, offices and laboratories of this biomedical research park, considered by many to be among the most important in Southern Europe.

La forma de este edificio es una de sus características más llamativas. Se trata de un cono truncado de planta elíptica de 117 x 74 metros, cortado a bisel y recubierto de madera. Esta estructura tiene un espacio central en forma de plaza, abierta ésta por la parte de menor altura del edificio, que se inclina en dirección al mar. Hacia el patio central asoman algunas circulaciones auxiliares, tras las que se encuentran los equipamientos, oficinas y laboratorios de este parque de investigación biomédica, considerado uno de los más importantes centros del sur de Europa.

L'une des caractéristiques les plus évidentes de ce bâtiment est sa forme. Il s'agit d'un cône tronqué sur une base élliptique de 117 x 74 mètres, coupé en biseau et recouvert de bois. Cette structure comporte un espace central en forme de place ouverte sur la partie la plus basse du bâtiment qui s'incline vers la mer. Quelques espaces de circulation secondaires débouchent sur la place centrale derrière laquelle se trouvent les équipements, bureaux et laboratoires de ce parc de recherche biomédicale. Il est considéré comme l'un des plus importants du sud de l'Europe.

La forma dell'edificio è una delle sue caratteristiche più vistose. Si tratta di un tronco di cono con una pianta ellittica di 117 x 74 metri, tagliato a bisello e rivestito in legno. La struttura presenta uno spazio centrale a forma di piazza, ricavato nel volume di minor altezza dell'edificio, che si inclina verso il mare. In direzione del cortile centrale affacciano diversi percorsi ausiliari di circolazione, dietro i quali si trovano le attrezzature, gli uffici e i laboratori di questo parco di ricerca biomedica, considerato come uno dei centri più importanti del sud d'Europa.

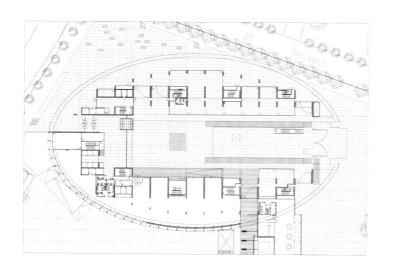

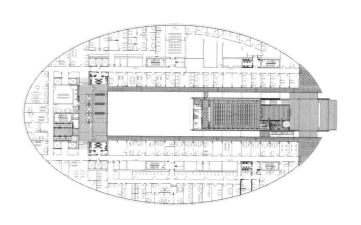

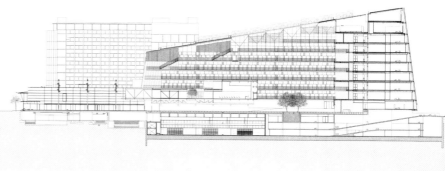

Capella García Arquitectura
Hotel Diagonal Barcelona | 2004
Avinguda Diagonal 205, 08018

Das Erdgeschoss dieses Hotels wirkt wie ein großes Aquarium. Die verschiedenen Körper und organischen Formen ahmen die visuelle Verformung von in Wasser eingetauchten Objekten nach. Das gewellte, aus Kreisformen bestehende Dach wirkt wie eine Wasserfläche, unter der sich die Rezeption, die verschiedenen Bereiche der Hall und die Bar in ihren jeweiligen, eigenen Konstruktionen befinden. Jede davon ist mit einem anderen Material (Kupfer, Holz und Kieselsteine) in Braun-, Gold- und Silbertönen verkleidet, womit ebenfalls wieder der Eindruck entsteht, dass es sich um einen futuristischen Meeresgrund handelt.

The ground floor of this hotel is inspired on a large aquarium. The different volumes and organic shapes emulate the visual distortion that affects objects when they are seen below water. The undulated roof made with circumferences represents the aquatic surface, below which we find reception; different areas of the *hall* and the bar are located in the small buildings. Each is covered in a different material like copper or wood, or the round edges which use shades of brown, silver and gold to achieve an original look, as if it were a futuristic sea bed.

La planta baja de este hotel está inspirada en un gran acuario. Los distintos volúmenes y las formas orgánicas emulan la distorsión visual que sufren los objetos sumergidos en el agua. El techo ondulado y formado por circunferencias representa la superficie acuática, bajo la que se encuentran la recepción, distintas zonas del *hall* y el bar, dispuestos en sus edículos. Cada uno está revestido de un material diferente como el cobre, la madera o los cantos rodados, que en tonos marrones, dorados y plata logran una estética original, como si de un futurista fondo marino se tratara.

Le rez-de-chaussée de cet hôtel s'inspire d'un grand aquarium. Les différents volumes ainsi que les formes organiques imitent la distortion visuelle à laquelle sont soumis les objets plongés dans l'eau. Le toit ondulé et composé de circonférences représente la surface de l'eau, sous laquelle se trouvent la réception, différentes zones du *hall* et le bar. Chacune indépendante des autres et revêtue d'un matériau différent, comme le cuivre ou le bois. Les galets aux tons divers, marrons, dorés et argentés, composent une esthétique originale suggérant un fond marin futuriste.

Il piano terreno di questo hotel è ispirato a un grande acquario. I diversi volumi e le forme organiche ricordano la distorsione visuale osservabile nei corpi sommersi in un liquido. La copertura ondulata e formata da circonferenze rappresenta la superficie dell'acqua, al di sotto della quale si trovano la reception, diverse zone dell'atrio e il bar, separati in zone riservate. Ognuno presenta un rivestimento differente: rame, legno o ciottoli naturali, con tonalità marroni, dorate e argento fuse in un ambiente dall'estetica originale che richiama alla mente un avveniristico fondale marino.

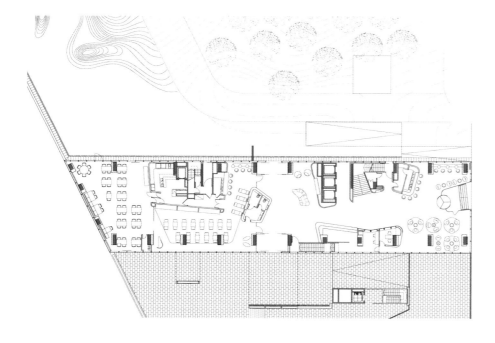

Carlos Ferrater
Botanical Institute of Barcelona | 2003
Passeig del Migdia s/n, 08038

Das Gebäude steht an einem Hang des Berges Montjuïc mit Blick auf einen großen Teil der Stadt. Seine horizontale Struktur stützt sich auf das Gelände im Urzustand, dessen Schräge man nutzte, um verschiedene, unabhängige Zugänge vom Garten und der hinteren Straße aus zu schaffen. Auf den drei Ebenen liegen ein Lager für Pflanzen und Bücher, das Museum Salvador und der dazugehörige Ausstellungssaal und ein Bereich, der den Wissenschaftlern vorbehalten ist. Für den Bau wurden die gleichen Materialien benutzt, die am Botanischen Garten verwendet wurden, z. B. unverkleideter Beton und Cortenstahl.

This building is located on the side of Montjuïc Mountain, a location from which one can see a large part of the city. Its horizontal structure is built on natural terrain, taking advantage of its slope to make various independent entrances from the garden and the road behind it. On its three levels one finds the plant deposits and library, the Salvador Museum –together with the exhibition hall– and an area reserved for scientists. It was built using materials already present in the Botanical Garden, such as exposed concrete and glazed porcelain.

El edificio está situado en la ladera de la montaña de Montjuïc, desde donde se divisa gran parte de la ciudad. Su estructura en horizontal reposa sobre el terreno natural, cuya pendiente ha sido aprovechada para disponer varios accesos independientes desde el jardín y la carretera posterior. En sus tres niveles se encuentran el depósito de plantas y libros, el Museo Salvador –junto a la sala de exposiciones– y un área restringida para científicos. Para su construcción se han usado materiales ya presentes en el Jardín Botánico, como el hormigón visto y el acero corten.

Le bâtiment est situé sur un des versants de la montagne de Montjuïc, depuis laquelle on peut voir une grande partie de la ville. Sa structure horizontale repose sur le terrain naturel, dont l'inclinaison a permis de disposer divers accès indépendants depuis le jardin et la route située à l'arrière. Sur trois niveaux on trouve la réserve de plantes et de livres, le musée Salvador –près de la salle d'expositions– et une zone réservée aux scientifiques. Des matériaux déjà présents dans le Jardin Botanique ont été utilisés pour sa construction, comme le béton apparent et l'acier corten.

L'edificio è situato su un fianco della montagna di Montjuïc, da cui si può osservare gran parte della città. La struttura orizzontale si adagia sul terreno naturale, la cui inclinazione è stata sfruttata per collocare diversi accessi indipendenti dal giardino e dalla strada sul retro. I tre livelli ospitano il deposito delle piante e dei libri, il Museo Salvador –assieme alla sala espositiva– e un'area riservata agli scienziati. Per la costruzione sono stati utilizzati materiali già presenti nel Giardino Botanico, come il calcestruzzo a vista e l'acciaio corten.

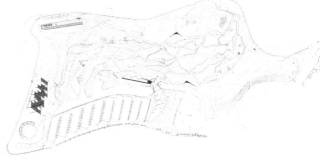

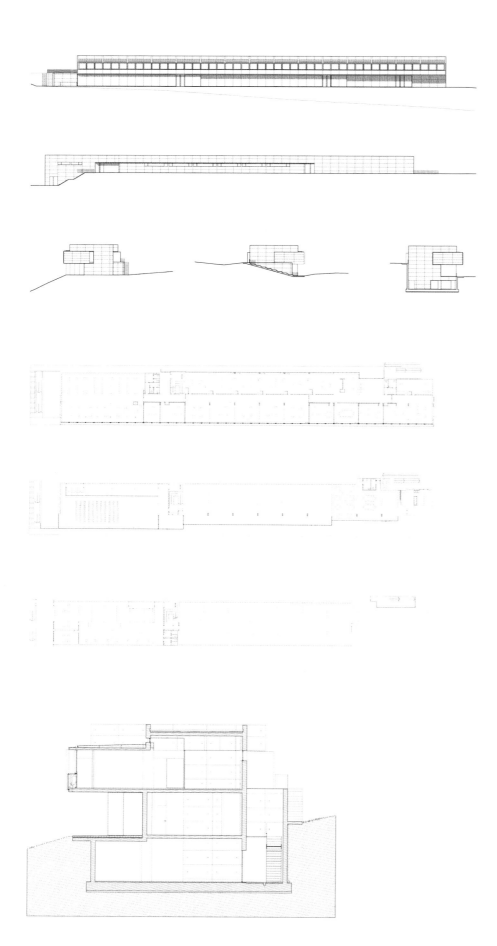

Carlos Ferrater
Social Services of Fort Pienc Neighborhood | 2004
Carretera Antiga d'Horta 1, 08013

Dieses im Inneren eines Häuserblocks gelegene Gebäude zeigt sich in einer sehr eigentümlichen Dualität. Von außen wirkt die Struktur sehr hermetisch, was durch die verwendeten Materialien Beton, Aluminium und das Zinkdach bewirkt wird, aber im Inneren wird so viel Licht wie möglich eingefangen. Die Teile, die das Gebäude bilden, werden durch das Licht, das in die Räume durch die Fenster, Dachfenster und Verglasungen an den Außenhöfen an beiden Seiten des Gebäudes einfällt, erhöht oder abgeflacht.

This building, located within an interior courtyard, presents a very characteristic duality. As opposed to the hermetic look of its exterior structure, which is achieved through materials like concrete, aluminum and a zinc cover, its interior seeks to capture as much light as possible. The pieces that form the building increase and decrease depending on the light entering through the windows, the skylights, and the glass that looks out towards the exterior patios located on either sides of the building.

Este edificio, ubicado en el interior de una manzana, presenta una dualidad muy característica. Frente al aspecto hermético que muestra en el exterior de su estructura, percepción reforzada por el uso de materiales como el hormigón, el aluminio o la cubierta de zinc, en su interior busca captar el máximo de luz posible. Las piezas que conforman el edificio crecen y decrecen en función de la luz que incide en los espacios interiores a través de las ventanas, los lucernarios y los vidrios de cara a los patios exteriores, situados a ambos lados del edificio.

Ce bâtiment, situé à l'intérieur d'un bloc de maisons, présente une dualité très singulière. Derrière l'aspect hermétique de l'extérieur, encore renforcé par l'utilisation de matériaux tels que le béton, l'aluminium ou le toit en zinc, l'intérieur est conçu pour capter un maximum de lumière. Les pièces constituant le bâtiment croissent et décroissent en fonction de la lumière qui pénètre dans les espaces intérieurs, à travers les fenêtres, les lucarnes et les carreaux donnant sur les cours extérieures, situées de chaque côté du bâtiment.

Questo edificio, ubicato all'interno di un isolato, presenta una dualità assai caratteristica. Rispetto all'aspetto ermetico percepibile all'esterno della struttura, sensazione rafforzata dall'uso di materiali come il calcestruzzo, l'alluminio o la copertura di zinco, l'interno cerca di catturare al massimo la luce naturale. Gli elementi che conformano l'edificio crescono e decrescono in funzione della luce che penetra negli spazi interni attraverso le finestre, i lucernari e le superfici vetrate che affacciano sui cortili esterni, situati lungo i due lati dell'edificio.

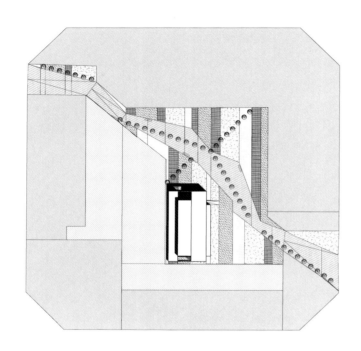

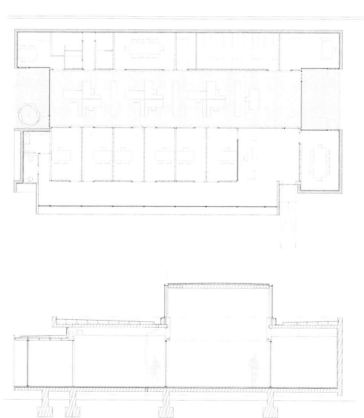

CCT Arquitectos
Julie Sohn Boutique | 2005
Diputació 229, 08007

Das neue Markenimage von Julie Sohn zeigt sich auch in der Gestaltung dieses Lokals, dessen U-Form eine Mansarde und ein Untergeschoss einschließt, so dass im gleichen Raum der Shop, der Showroom und das Atelier untergebracht sind. Durch den Abriss der Zwischenwände und der doppelten Decken wurde die Originalstruktur mit ihren Ziegelwänden und Eisenträgern wieder sichtbar gemacht. In einer eingezogenen Decke der Form umgedrehter Pyramiden mit einer rhomben- und trapezförmigen Basis wurden die Installationen verborgen. Zur Ausstellung der Teile wurden Platten aus weiß lackiertem Holz entworfen, die wie Bilder aufgehängt sind und verschiedene Kompositionen schaffen.

Julie Sohn's new image is reflected in the design of this boutique, which has a U shape that includes an attic and basement, bringing the boutique, the showroom and the studio together in a single space. By knocking down walls and false ceilings, they've left the original structure visible, with brick walls, wood beams and iron pillars. The false ceiling consisting of inverted pyramids with rhomboidal and trapezoidal bases allows them to hide the electrical installation. To expose pieces they designed white-lacquered wood soffits that hang like paintings and create different compositions.

La nueva imagen de Julie Sohn se refleja en el diseño de este local, cuya forma en U incluye un altillo y un sótano, lo que unifica en un mismo espacio la tienda, el *showroom* y el estudio. El derribo de los tabiques y falsos techos deja la estructura original a la vista, con paredes de ladrillos, vigas y pilares de hierro. El falso techo difusor de pirámides invertidas de base romboidal y trapezoidal permite esconder las instalaciones. Para exponer las piezas se diseñaron plafones de madera lacada en blanco, que cuelgan a modo de cuadros y crean diferentes composiciones.

La nouvelle image de Julie Sohn se reflète dans la conception de ce lieu, dont la forme en U comporte une mezzanine et un sous-sol, ce qui réunit la boutique, le *showroom* et le studio dans un espace unique. La supression des murs et des faux plafonds laisse apparaître la structure originelle : des murs de briques, des poutres et des colonnes en fer. Le faux plafond diffuseur constitué de pyramides inversées en forme de trapèze ou de losange, permet de cacher les équipements. Pour exposer les pièces, des plafonniers en bois laqué blanc ont été conçus. Ils pendent tels des tableaux créant ainsi des compositions diverses.

La nuova immagine di Julie Sohn si riflette nel design di questo locale, il cui volume a forma di U accoglie un soppalco e uno scantinato, riunendo nello stesso spazio la boutique, lo *showroom* e lo studio. La demolizione dei tramezzi e dei controsoffitti lascia la struttura originale a vista, con pareti in mattoni, travi e pilastri di ferro. Il controsoffitto diffusore con piramidi inverse a base romboidale e trapezoidale nasconde alla vista gli impianti. Per l'esposizione dei capi sono stati disegnati degli elementi in legno laccato bianco che, appesi come fossero quadri, creano differenti composizioni.

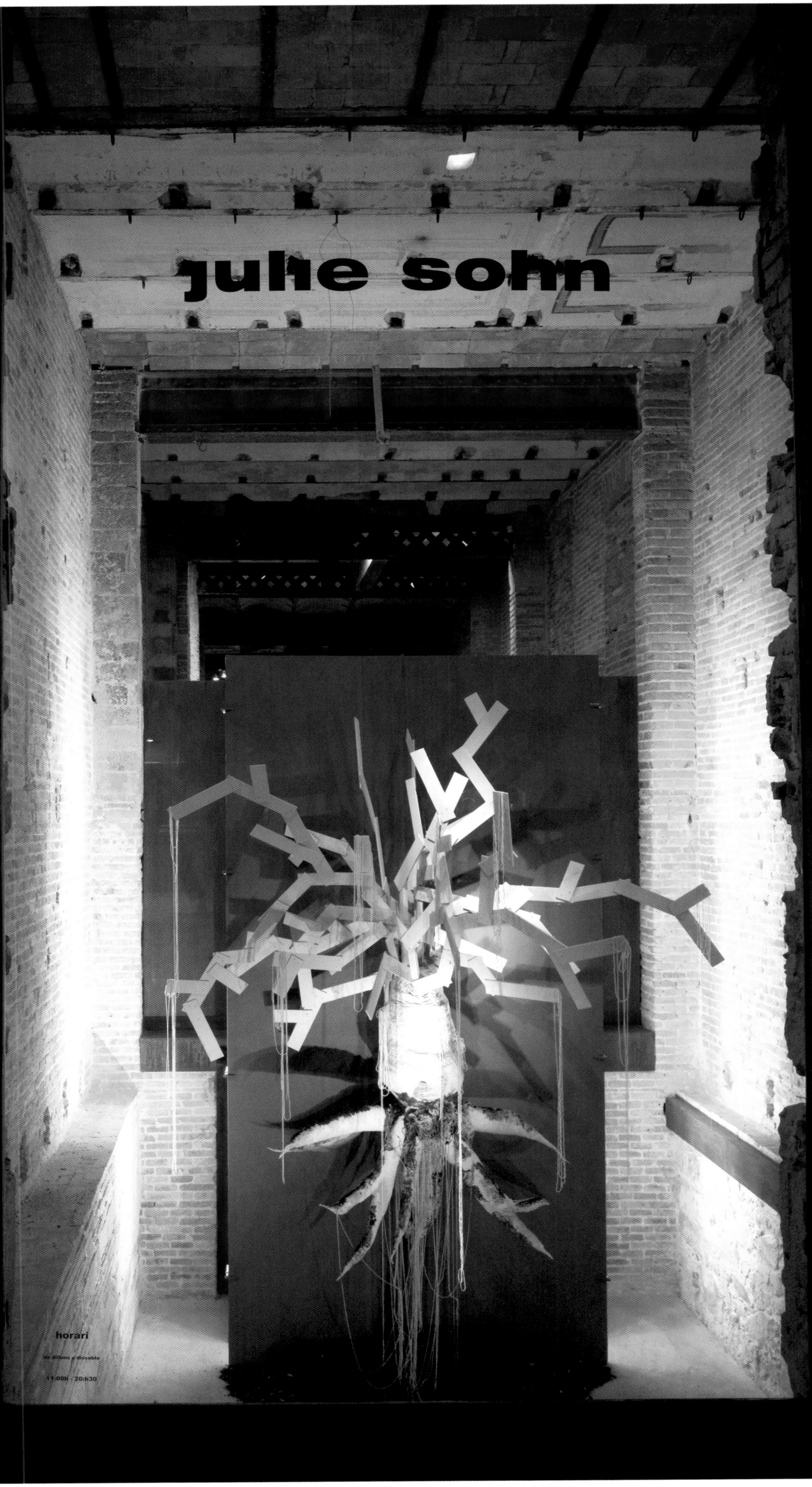
julie sohn
horari
de dilluns a dissabte
11:00h - 20:h30

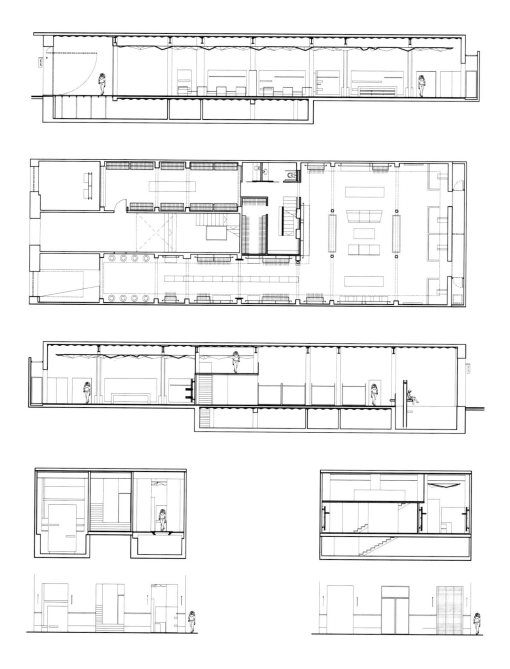

Clotet, Paricio i Associats/Lluís Clotet, Ignasi Paricio
Illa de la Llum | 2005
Passeig de Garcia Fària 73-77, 08019

Die Ästhetik der Fassade dieses Gebäudes, das 230 Wohnungen beherbergt, wird durch die drei verschieden hohen Türme mit 26, 18 und 5 Stockwerken geprägt. Es wird ganz deutlich auf schlanke Formen bei den Gebäuden verzichtet; der Schwerpunkt liegt darauf, die Stockwerke so gut wie möglich auszunutzen, um Wohnungen verschiedener Größen und mit verschiedenen Aufteilungen zu schaffen. Die Schiebejalousien aus Aluminium wiederholen sich an der ganzen Fassade wie kleine, mobile Teile eines Puzzles. Von den großen Terrassen hat man einen wundervollen Blick auf das Meer und die Zone des Forums.

It's impossible not to notice the facade of this building with 230 homes, formed by three towers of different heights, with 26, 18 and 5 floors, respectively. The project clearly renounces the obsession for the slenderness of its buildings, and focuses on maximizing space throughout the planning of homes of different shapes and sizes. The aluminum sliding venetian blinds are repeated throughout its façade, like small mobile *puzzle* pieces. Their large terraces offer unmatchable views of the sea and Forum area.

Es inevitable recaer en la estética de la fachada de este edificio de 230 viviendas, formado por tres torres de diferentes alturas, con 26, 18 y 5 plantas respectivamente. El proyecto renuncia claramente a la obsesión por la esbeltez de los edificios, dirige su atención a aprovechar al máximo la ocupación en planta para planear viviendas de diferentes tamaños y distribuciones. Las persianas correderas de aluminio se repiten por toda la fachada, como pequeñas piezas móviles de un *puzzle*. Sus amplias terrazas ofrecen inigualables vistas al mar y a la zona del Fórum.

Il est impossible de ne pas évoquer la façade de ce bâtiment de 230 logements, composé de trois tours de différentes hauteurs de 26, 18 et 5 étages respectivement. Le projet renonce délibérément à l'obsession de minceur des bâtiments actuels. Il vise plutôt à occuper au mieux l'espace disponible pour élaborer des appartements de différentes tailles, comme s'il s'agissait des pièces d'un *puzzle*. Ses terrasses offrent une vue imprenable sur la mer et la zone du Forum.

È inevitabile soffermarsi sull'estetica della facciata di questo edificio di 230 abitazioni, formato da tre torri di differente altezza, con 26, 18 e 5 livelli rispettivamente. Il progetto rinuncia chiaramente all'ossessione per le geometrie slanciate degli edifici e centra l'attenzione sul massimo sfruttamento delle superfici calpestabili dando vita a residenze di differenti dimensioni e distribuzione. I serramenti scorrevoli in alluminio si ripetono lungo tutta la superficie esterna, come piccoli pezzi mobili di un puzzle. Le ampie terrazze offrono viste ineguagliabili verso il mare e la zona del Forum.

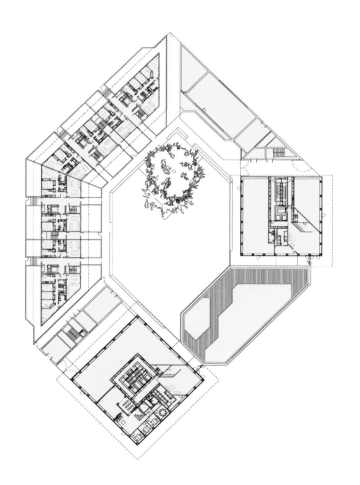

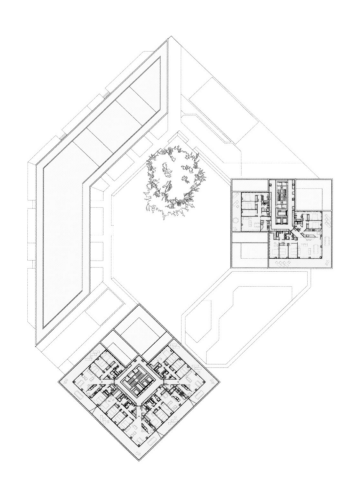

EMBT/Enric Miralles-Benedetta Tagliabue

Gas Natural Headquarters | 2005

Plaça del Gas 1, 08003

Das Grundstück, auf dem dieser Gebäudekomplex steht, ist das gleiche, auf dem vor 160 Jahren das erste Gaswerk Spaniens entstand. Das Gebäude besteht aus drei Elementen: dem verglasten Turm, aus dem auf spektakuläre Weise eine über dem Boden schwebende Struktur herausragt, in der sich fünf Stockwerke befinden, und einem ebenfalls verglasten Anbau mit der Form eines Wasserfalls. Durch die verschiedenartigen und originellen Formen hebt sich das Gebäude von den anliegenden Häusern ab, integriert sich aber unter architektonischen Gesichtspunkten gut ins Stadtbild.

The location of this complex is precisely where Spain's first gas factory was founded 160 years ago. The construction is composed of three elements: the glass tower from which juts out a spectacular projection that goes from the fifth to the tenth floors, and a third piece, which is also made of glass and takes the shape of a cascade. The variety and originality of its volumes make this headquarters stand out among the buildings around it, while at the same time, integrating itself with the city from an architectural point of view.

Los terrenos en los que se encuentra este complejo son los mismos donde hace 160 años se instaló la primera fábrica de gas de España. La construcción está compuesta por tres elementos: la torre acristalada de la que sobresale un espectacular voladizo que ocupa de la quinta a la décima planta y una tercera pieza, un anexo también acristalado y en forma de cascada. La variedad y originalidad de su volumetría hacen que la sede destaque entre los edificios colindantes, al tiempo que logra integrarse a la ciudad desde un punto de vista arquitectónico.

Les terrains sur lesquels se trouve ce complexe sont les mêmes qui ont accueilli, il y a plus de 160 ans, la première usine de gaz d'Espagne. La construction se compose de trois éléments : la tour en verre de laquelle surgit une saillie spectaculaire allant du cinquième au dizième étage et enfin, une troisième partie également en verre en forme de cascade. La variété et l'originalité de ses volumes font que le bâtiment se distingue de ceux qui l'entourent, tout en s'intégrant parfaitement à la ville du point de vue architectural.

I terreni che accolgono questo complesso sono gli stessi in cui, 160 anni fa, è stata installata la prima fabbrica di gas della Spagna. La costruzione è composta da tre elementi: la torre vetrata dalla quale si proietta uno spettacolare aggetto che occupa dal quinto al decimo livello, e un terzo volume, un annesso vetrato a forma di cascata. Il complesso spicca nell'immediato contesto per la varietà e l'originalità della sua volumetria, ma riesce sicuramente ad integrarsi alla città da un punto di vista architettonico.

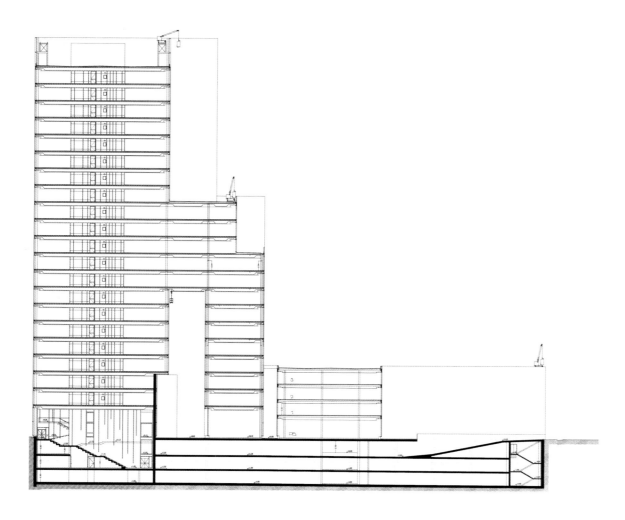

EMBT/Enric Miralles-Benedetta Tagliabue

Restoration of Santa Caterina Market | 2005
Avinguda de Francesc Cambó 16, 08003

Unter den kräftigen Farben des Keramikdachs des Markts, die die Farbigkeit des feilgebotenen Obsts und Gemüses nachahmen, verbirgt sich das Ergebnis einer sorgfältig geplanten Instandsetzung. Es mussten Lösungen für diesen komplexen Standort gefunden werden, die den täglichen Kunden- und Besucherfluss erleichtern. Deshalb wurde der mittlere Bereich abgerissen und in Originalgröße mit Holzstrukturen neu errichtet, die den Übergang aus der zentralen Halle in die Vorhallen erleichtern und draußen schattige Zonen schaffen.

Beneath the market's colorful ceramic rooftop, which emulates the colors of fruits and vegetables, we can see the result of a very well-planned reconstruction project. The aim was to provide solutions for the area's complexity, namely its location and the need to facilitate the steady flow of customers and daily deliveries. To do this they knocked down the central area and reconstructed the original perimeter with wood structures that ease the transition from the central hall to the porches and provide a shaded outdoor area.

Bajo los llamativos colores de la cubierta de cerámica del mercado, que emulan el colorido de las frutas y verduras, se halla el resultado de un cuidadoso proyecto de rehabilitación. El objetivo era aportar soluciones a la complejidad del lugar, a su ubicación y facilitar así el flujo de gente y mercancías diario. Por este motivo se derribó la parte central y se reconstruyó el perímetro original con estructuras de madera que facilitan la transición de la sala central a los porches y logran una zona sombreada en el exterior.

Sous les couleurs vives du toit en céramique du marché, rappelant celles des fruits et des légumes, on peut admirer le travail minutieux du projet de réhabilitation. Il s'agissait de résoudre les problèmes dus à la complexité du lieu ainsi qu'à son emplacement et faciliter le flux quotidien de personnes et de marchandises. La partie centrale à donc été détruite et le périmètre originel reconstruit avec des structures en bois favorisant la transition entre la salle centrale et les porches, créant de fait une zone ombragée à l'extérieur.

Sotto i vistosi colori della copertura in ceramica del mercato, che richiamano le tonalità della frutta e della verdura, si trova il risultato di un meticoloso progetto di riabilitazione. L'obiettivo era quello di apportare soluzioni alla complessità del luogo e della sua ubicazione, e facilitare in questo modo la circolazione diaria delle persone e della merce. Per questo motivo è stata demolita la parte centrale e il perimetro originale è stato ricostruito con strutture in legno che agevolano la transizione dalla sala centrale ai portici creando inoltre una zona esterna all'ombra.

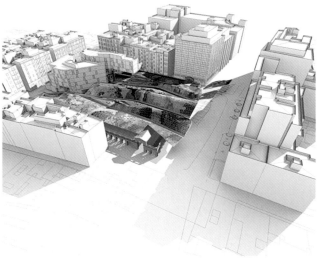

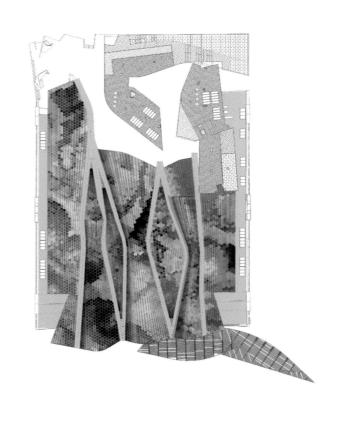

Futur-2
Sugar Club | 2004
Moll de Barcelona s/n. World Trade Center, 08039

Von diesem Lokal aus hat man einen unvergleichlichen Blick auf den beliebten Hafen von Barcelona, mittlerweile zu einem der Wahrzeichen der Stadt geworden. Der Sugar Club liegt im Erdgeschoss des World Trade Centers direkt am Meer und teilt sich in unterschiedliche Bereiche auf, Cafeteria, Restaurant, Cocktailbar und Lounge Club. Man kann diese wunderschöne Lage und den Panoramablick durch die großen Fenster zu jeder Tageszeit in einer modernen und avantgardistisch gestalteten Umgebung genießen.

This place has the privilege of offering one of the best views of the busy and emblematic port of Barcelona. Located on the ground floor of the World Trade Center business complex, just beside the sea, Sugar Club offers a wide range to choose from, including a café and restaurant, a cocktail bar and lounge club. Its exceptional location and large glass windows offers panoramic views that can be enjoyed at any hour of the day, in an atmosphere decorated with modern and avant-garde esthetics.

Este local tiene el privilegio de ofrecer una de las mejores vistas hacia el concurrido y emblemático puerto de Barcelona. Situado en la parte baja del centro de negocios World Trade Center, justo al lado del mar, el Sugar Club cuenta con un amplio abanico de propuestas que incluye cafetería y restaurante, coctelería y lounge club. Así, su excepcional ubicación y sus vistas panorámicas, a través de grandes cristaleras, se pueden disfrutar a cualquier hora del día, en un ambiente cuya decoración responde a una estética moderna y vanguardista.

Ce lieu a le privilège d'offrir l'une des meilleures vues sur le très prisé et très emblématique port de Barcelone. Situé dans la partie inférieure du centre d'affaires World Trade Center, en bord de mer, le Sugar Club dispose d'un large éventail d'offres incluant une cafétéria et un restaurant, une cocktailerie et un lounge club. On peut ainsi profiter de sa situation exceptionnelle et de ses vues panoramiques, grâce à de larges baies vitrées, à toute heure de la journée, dans une ambiance dont la décoration correspond à une esthétique moderne et avant-garde.

Il locale si colloca in una posizione privilegiata e offre una delle migliori viste verso l'animato ed emblematico porto di Barcellona. Situato nella parte inferiore del centro affaristico del World Trade Center, accanto al mare, lo Sugar Club dispone di una vasta gamma di proposte e accoglie una caffetteria con ristorante, cocktail bar e lounge club. Data l'eccezionale ubicazione, è possibile godere delle viste panoramiche attraverso le grandi vetrate durante l'intero arco della giornata, in un ambiente decorato secondo un'estetica moderna e all'avanguardia.

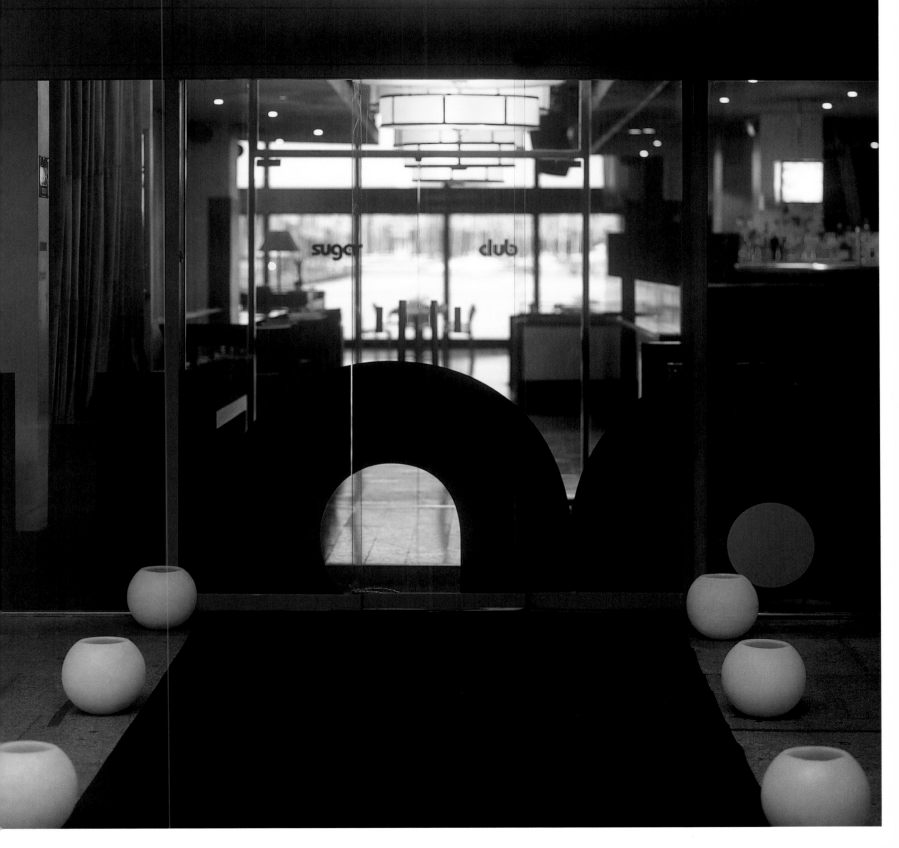

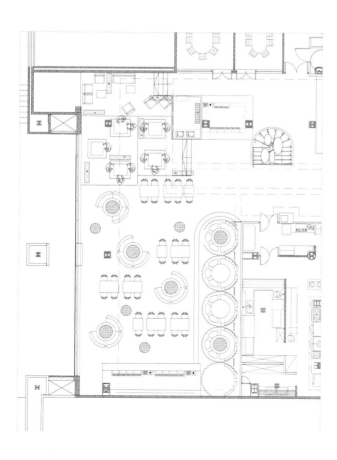

GCA Arquitectes Associats
Evo Restaurant | 2006
Gran Via 144, 08907 L'Hospitalet

Dieses Restaurant liegt auf 105 Metern Höhe in einer verglasten Kuppel, die das Hotel Hesperia Tower krönt, so dass die Gäste einen wundervollen Blick über einen großen Teil der Stadt haben. Die komplexe Innengestaltung verbindet das spektakuläre Design der Architekten Richard Rogers und Alonso & Balaguer mit der hochwertigen Qualität der Küche des Küchenchefs Santi Santamaría. Dazu wurden kreisförmige Plattformen auf verschiedenen Ebenen geschaffen, die den Durchgang erleichtern und private, persönliche Bereiche für die Tische entstehen lassen.

Situated 344 feet up in the air, this restaurant is located in the glass cupola that crowns the Hotel Hesperia Tower, offering dinners views of a large part of the city. The complexity of its interior design resides in combining the spectacular nature of the architectural space created by Richard Rogers and Alonso & Balaguer with maximum enjoyment provided by the top-quality cuisine of Chef Santi Santamaría. They achieved this by creating circular platforms at different levels, which allows for movement, while providing privacy and giving each of the tables its own identity.

Los 105 metros de altura en los que se encuentra este restaurante, situado en la cúpula acristalada que corona el Hotel Hesperia Tower, ofrecen a los comensales unas vistas que alcanzan gran parte de la ciudad. La complejidad del diseño interior reside en conciliar la espectacularidad del espacio arquitectónico de la mano de Richard Rogers y Alonso & Balaguer con el máximo disfrute de la calidad de la alta cocina del chef Santi Santamaría. Por ello se crearon plataformas circulares a distintos niveles, que resuelven la circulación y aportan privacidad e identidad en la ubicación de las mesas.

Ce restaurant situé à une hauteur de 105 mètres, dans la coupole de verre qui surmonte l'Hôtel Hesperia Tower, offre aux convives des vues exceptionnelles de toute la ville. La complexité du design intérieur réside dans la difficulté de concilier l'espace architectural spectaculaire, oeuvre de Richard Rogers et Alonso & Balaguer, et le plaisir sans partage que procure la grande cuisine du chef Santi Santamaría. C'est la raison pour laquelle des plateformes circulaires ont été créées sur plusieurs niveaux, organisant ainsi la circulation tout en conservant l'intimité et l'identité du lieu où l'on mange.

Questo ristorante è situato a 105 metri d'altezza, nella cupola di vetro che corona l'Hotel Hesperia Tower, e offre ai commensali delle viste che abbracciano gran parte della città. All'interno, la complessità del design risiede nel conciliare la spettacolarità dello spazio architettonico creato da Richard Rogers e Alonso & Balaguer con la possibilità di gustare al massimo la qualità dei piatti di alta cucina dello chef Santi Santamaría. Per questo lo spazio presenta piattaforme circolari a diversi livelli che risolvono la circolazione apportando privacy e identità in quanto all'ubicazione dei tavoli.

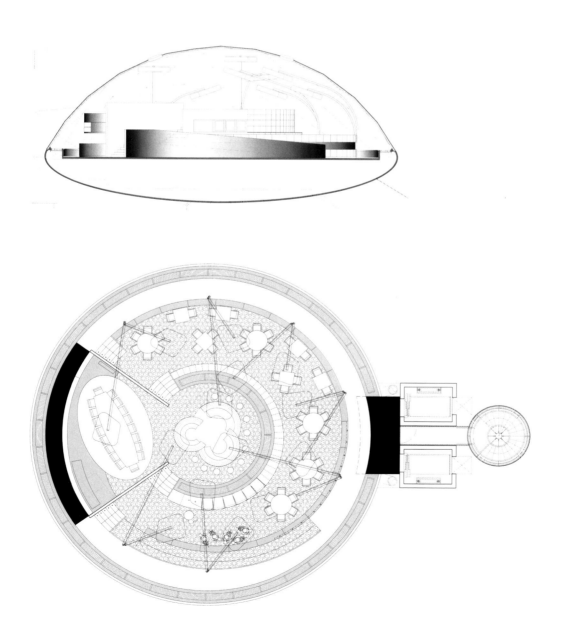

GCA Arquitectes Associats

Olivia Plaza Hotel | 2007
Plaça de Catalunya 19, 08002

Dieses Hotel befindet sich an einem besonders exklusiven Standort, nämlich an der berühmten Plaça de Catalunya. Die Terrasse im Inneren ist von den Ruinen der ehemaligen Stadtmauer umgeben. Im Erdgeschoss liegen die mit einer modernen und zeitgemäßen Zen-Ästhetik gestalteten Gemeinschaftsbereiche des Hotels. In die Zimmer wurde ein Teil des Bads integriert, und zwar durch ein großes Möbel aus MDF-Platten, das fast wie eine Skulptur wirkt.

The exclusive location of this hotel, in the famous Plaça de Catalunya, makes it a privileged enclave. Looking no further, the terrace you find in its courtyards is surrounded by archaeological remains of the city walls. On the ground floor we find common areas boasting a contemporary and modern design with zen esthetics. The rooms have been designed by integrating part of the bathroom, accomplished with a design that makes an almost sculptural piece of furniture out of MD.

La exclusiva ubicación de este hotel, en la famosa Plaça de Catalunya, lo convierte en un enclave privilegiado. Sin ir más lejos, la terraza que se encuentra en el interior está rodeada por los restos arqueológicos de la muralla. En la planta baja se sitúan las zonas comunes diseñadas en un estilo contemporáneo y moderno tintado de estética zen. Las habitaciones se han diseñado integrando en ellas parte del lavabo, cuyo diseño se resuelve en un gran mueble de DM que es casi una pieza escultórica.

La situation privilégiée de cet hôtel, sur la célèbre Plaça de Catalunya, en fait un lieu très spécial. La terrasse intérieure est entourée des restes archéologiques d'une muraille. Au rez-de-chaussée se trouvent les zones communes conçues dans un style contemporain et moderne teinté d'esthétique zen. Les chambres intègrent une partie de la salle de bains dont le design se fond dans un grand meuble de DM, une pièce sculpturale à lui seul.

Data l'esclusiva ubicazione, nella famosa Plaça de Catalunya, l'hotel si colloca in una posizione privilegiata. Solo per fare un esempio, la terrazza che accoglie al suo interno è circondata dai resti archeologici della muraglia. Il piano terreno ospita le zone comuni, in stile contemporaneo e moderno con un tocco di estetica zen. Le camere sono state disegnate integrandovi un lavabo, un grande mobile di DM collocato al loro interno quasi come un'opera scultorea.

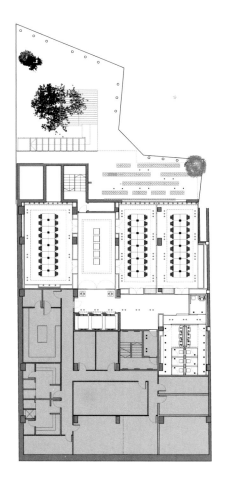

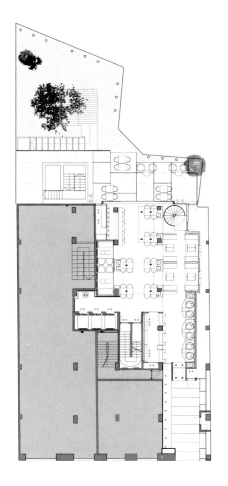

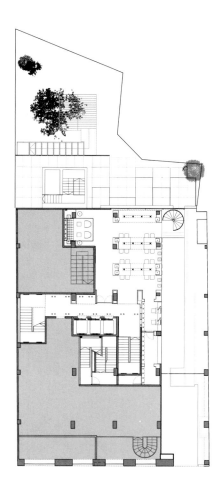

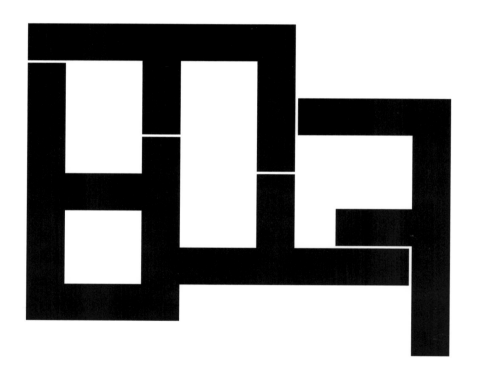

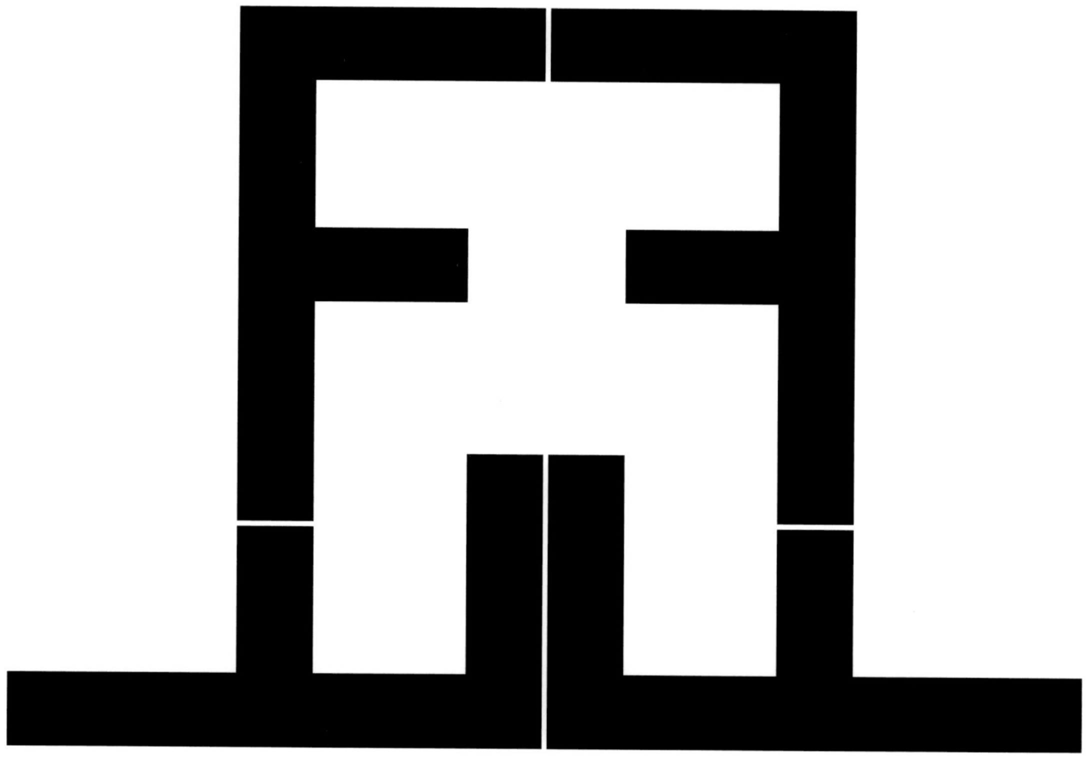

GCA Arquitectes Associats
Oriol Balaguer's Cake Shop | 2005
Morales 21-27, 08029

Der schwarz gestrichene Metallrahmen der Fassade bildet eine betonte Grenze zwischen dem Inneren und dem Äußeren des Shops. Zwei hängende Tabletts aus Platinen aus mattem Stahl sind die einzigen Ausstellungselemente im Schaufenster, eine minimalistische Lösung, die mit dem Interieur in Einklang steht, das wie eine Kiste aus im Siebdruck bedruckten Spiegeln gestaltet ist, in der sich Bilder und Farben mischen. Die Möbelstücke wirken wie Skulpturen, die aus dem Boden und den Wänden ragen. Sie lassen den Raum sehr einheitlich wirken.

The black metallic frame on the facade creates a strong contrast between the shop's interior and exterior. Two hanging matt platinum metal trays are all that's displayed in the shop window, a minimalist solution that matches its interior, conceived as a silk-screen mirror box that combines images and colors. The furniture elements are sculptural pieces that come out of the floor and walls, helping to achieve uniformity in its design.

El marco metálico pintado en negro de la fachada crea una fuerte demarcación entre el interior y el exterior de la tienda. Dos bandejas colgantes en pletina de acero mate se convierten en los únicos expositores del escaparate, una solución minimalista acorde con el interior, concebido como una caja de espejo serigrafiado donde se mezclan las imágenes y los colores. Los elementos de mobiliario son piezas escultóricas que sobresalen del suelo y las paredes, con lo que se consigue una percepción de uniformidad en el diseño.

Le cadre métallique peint en noir de la façade établit une limite marquée entre l'intérieur et l'extérieur du magasin. Deux plateaux en plétine d'acier mat suspendus dans les vitrines sont les seules pièces exposées. Une solution minimaliste en accord avec l'intérieur, conçu comme une boîte miroir sérigraphiée dans laquelle les images et les couleurs s'entremêlent. Le mobilier est constitué d'éléments sculpturaux surgissant du sol et des murs grâce auxquels le design gagne en cohérence.

La struttura metallica dipinta in nero che caratterizza la facciata crea una forte separazione tra l'interno e l'esterno del negozio. Due vassoi sospesi di acciaio opaco sono gli unici espositori della vetrina, una soluzione minimalista in armonia con l'interno, concepito come una scatola di specchio serigrafato in cui si mescolano immagini e colori. Gli elementi dell'arredo sono pezzi scultorei che spuntano dal suolo e dalle pareti, e riescono a conferire armonia e uniformità al design.

126

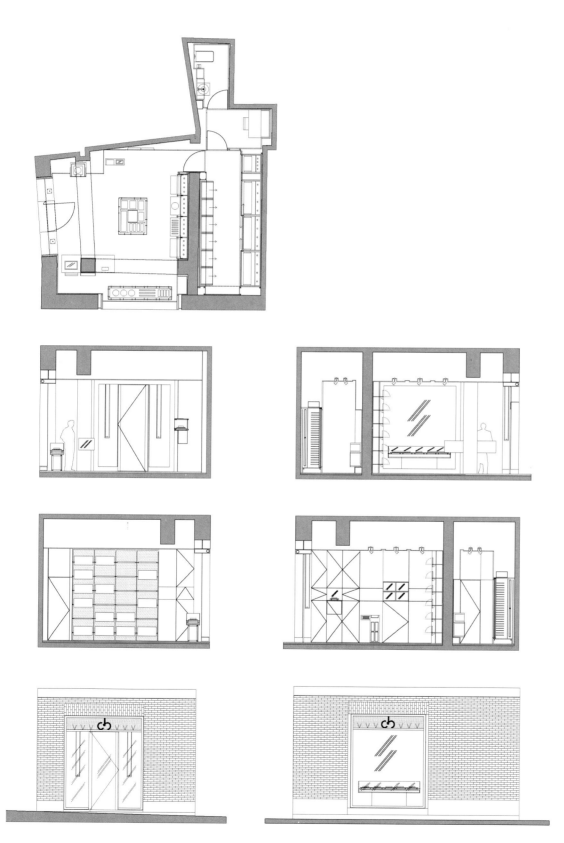

GCA Arquitectes Associats
QK Boutique | 2007
Calvet 29, 08021

Oft werden auf der Suche nach neuen Trends Stile anderer Epochen wieder aufgegriffen. Der Shop QK ist eine Hommage an den „Barockismus", an die Formen des Barocks. Man setzte auf edle Formen, um einen würdigen Hintergrund für die Kollektionen zu schaffen. Durch die Verwendung von Materialien mit verschiedenen Texturen und Formen und die ständige Präsenz der Farbe Schwarz zwischen Metall und Glas wurde eine moderne Ästhetik geschaffen. Die sorgfältig gewählte, betörende und hochwertige Beleuchtung zeigt die Kleidungsstücke und Accessoires.

Often the search for new tendencies provokes styles from other eras to be given another look. The QK Boutique pays homage to the Baroque, seeking sophistication in shape while creating a backdrop for their collections. The use of materials with different textures and shapes, as well as the omnipresence of the color black among materials like shiny metal and glass, gives it a modern air. The careful attention to the lighting, which is enveloping and of refined taste, illuminates clothing items and accessories.

A menudo, la búsqueda de nuevas tendencias suscita la revisión de estilos de otras épocas. En la tienda QK se ha rendido homenaje al barroquismo, se ha apostado por la sofisticación de sus formas para crear el telón de fondo de las colecciones. El uso de materiales con diferentes texturas y formas, así como la constante presencia del color negro entre los brillos de metales y cristales, logran una estética moderna. La cuidada iluminación, envolvente y sofisticada, muestra las piezas de ropa y complementos.

Il arrive souvent que la recherche de nouvelles tendances nous fasse revisiter des époques passées. Dans le magasin QK c'est au baroque qu'il est rendu hommage. La sophistification de ses formes a servi à créer la toile de fond pour les collections. L'utilisation de matériaux aux textures et formes diverses, ainsi que la présence constante du noir entre les éclats des métaux et des cristaux, réussi à créer une esthétique moderne. L'éclairage soigné, enveloppant et sophistiqué, met en valeur les vêtements et les accessoires.

Spesso, la ricerca di nuove tendenze porta alla revisione di stili tipici di altre epoche. La boutique QK rende omaggio al barocchismo affidandosi alla sofisticazione delle forme nella creazione dello sfondo più adatto per le sue collezioni. L'uso di materiali con differenti forme e qualità tattili e la costante presenza del nero tra le superfici brillanti di vetro e di metallo danno vita a un insieme caratterizzato da un'estetica moderna. L'elaborata illuminazione, avvolgente e sofisticata, mette in risalto i capi d'abbigliamento e gli accessori.

Herzog & de Meuron
Forum Building | 2004
Rambla de Prim 2-4, 08019

Dieses Gebäude entstand ebenfalls im Zuge der urbanistischen Neugestaltung am Ende der Allee Diagonal am Meer. Die Basis des Gebäudes ist ein gleichseitiges Dreieck, 180 Meter lang und 25 Meter hoch. Die unebene Fassade ist mit meeresblauem Farbpulver bedeckt und wird von verschiedenen vertikalen, reflektierenden Fenstern durchzogen, die den Fall von Wasser nachahmen. Die Struktur, an der die Waagerechte betont wurde, um eine größere funktionelle Flexibilität zu erreichen, ist an 17 Punkten aufgehängt und scheint in der Luft zu schweben. Darunter entstand ein überdachter Platz zur Straße, der frei zugänglich ist.

This building forms part of the city-planning makeover that was implemented at the end of Diagonal Avenue, where it meets the sea. The building's foundation is an 82 foot high, 590 foot equilateral triangle, with a wavy, navy blue façade that is interrupted by various vertical reflecting windows that emulate water falling. This structure, which was projected by reinforcing its horizontalness to achieve greater flexibility in its functions, hangs suspended in air by 17 support points, thus creating a covered area of public space down on the street.

Este edificio forma parte de la regeneración urbanística llevada a cabo al final de la avenida Diagonal, frente al mar. La base del edificio es un triángulo equilátero de 180 metros de lado y 25 de altura, con una fachada rugosa pulverizada de color azul ultramar y atravesada por varias ventanas reflectantes verticales que emulan la caída del agua. Esta estructura, proyectada con el refuerzo de su horizontalidad para lograr mayor flexibilidad en sus funciones, queda suspendida en el aire por 17 puntos de apoyo que crean un espacio cubierto de uso público en la calle.

Ce bâtiment fait partie de la réhabilitation urbanistique menée à la fin de l'avenue Diagonal, face à la mer. La base de l'édifice est un triangle équilatéral de 180 mètres de côté pour 25 mètres de haut. Sa façade est rugueuse, saupoudrée de bleu outremer et traversée verticalement par plusieurs verrières réfléchissantes imitant la chute de l'eau. Cette structure, tirant profit de son horizontalité pour une plus grande flexibilité dans son utilisation, est suspendue en l'air par 17 points d'appui créant un espace public couvert au niveau de la rue.

L'edificio si inserisce nel programma di rinnovamento urbanistico realizzato al termine della Diagonal, di fronte al mare. La base della struttura è un triangolo equilatero di 180 metri di lato e 25 d'altezza, con una facciata rugosa e polverizzata in azzurro oltremare, attraversata da diverse vetrate verticali riflettenti che imitano la caduta dell'acqua. Con l'intenzione di conseguire una maggiore funzionalità, il progetto sfrutta l'orizzontalità della struttura, che si sostiene su 17 punti d'appoggio staccandosi dal terreno e creando uno spazio pubblico coperto al livello della strada.

Jaime Hayón
Camper Store | 2007
Passeig de Gràcia 30, 08007

Der Designer Jaime Hayón hat mit viel Phantasie und Kreativität diesen neuen Shop entworfen, eine persönliche Interpretation der Welt von Camper, in der sich das Konzept Laden-Galerie entwickelt hat. Dieser Designer zeigt eine gewisse Vorliebe für die Handarbeit, ohne sich dabei jedoch vollständig von den neuen Technologien abzuwenden. Dies spiegelt sich in den Möbeln und Dekorationsstücken wieder, alle von großer Qualität. Sie beweisen, dass Tradition und Modernität nicht unvereinbar sind. Die Räume sind voller Farben, die Schuhe scheinen einen Teil der Dekoration zu bilden.

Designer Jaime Hayón has made use of all his fantasy and creativity in order to project this new store, a personal interpretation of the Camper universe which has developed the concept of store-gallery. His predilection for manual labor, without turning his back completely on new technologies, is noticeable in the furniture and accessories, pieces of great-quality that show that tradition and modernity are not completely at odds. In this colorful space, the shoes look like they form part of the decoration.

El diseñador Jaime Hayón ha echado mano de toda su fantasía y creatividad para proyectar esta nueva tienda, una personal interpretación del universo Camper en el que se ha desarrollado el concepto de tienda-galería. La predilección del creativo por el trabajo manual, aunque sin dar la espalda totalmente a las nuevas tecnologías, se hace notable en los muebles y complementos, piezas de gran calidad que demuestran que la tradición y la modernidad no están del todo reñidas. En este espacio lleno de color, los zapatos parecen formar parte de la decoración.

Le designer Jaime Hayón a fait appel à toute sa fantaisie et à toute sa créativité pour la conception de cette nouvelle boutique. Il s'agit d'une interprétation toute personnelle de l'univers de Camper dans le cadre duquel s'est développé le concept de boutique-galerie. La prédilection du designer pour le travail manuel, sans toutefois tourner totalement le dos aux nouvelles technologies, s'apprécie sutout dans les meubles et les accessoires, des pièces de grande qualité démontrant que la modernité et la tradition ne sont pas totalement incompatibles. Dans cet espace plein de couleurs, les chaussures semblent faire partie du décor.

Il designer Jaime Hayón ha fatto appello a tutta la sua fantasia e a tutta la sua creatività per il progetto di questo nuovo negozio, una personale interpretazione dell'universo Camper in cui è stato sviluppato il concetto di boutique-galleria. La predilezione dell'artista per il lavoro manuale, ma senza voltare completamente le spalle alle nuove tecnologie, si fa notare nei mobili e negli accessori, elementi di gran qualità che dimostrano che tradizione e modernità non sono del tutto incompatibili. In questo spazio pieno di colore, le scarpe sembrano far parte della decorazione.

Jordi Tió, Ferran Amat (interior design)
Hotel Casa Camper | 2004
Elisabets 11, 08001

Auf den ersten Blick könnte man dieses Hotel mit einem Fahrradgeschäft oder einer Kunstgalerie verwechseln. Die Originalstruktur des Gebäudes, die man erhalten hat, bildet einen Gegensatz zu den modern und avantgardistisch eingerichteten Interieurs, in denen die Farben Rot, Weiß und Schwarz vorherrschen. In den Fluren und an den Türen fallen die persönlich gestalteten Symbole auf, die exklusiv für das Hotel entworfen wurden. Einzelheiten wie das große Wandgemälde von Hannah Collins mitten im Speisezimmer, das Fassaden einiger alter Geschäfte des Viertels zeigt, erinnern daran, dass sich das Hotel mitten im historischen Stadtkern befindet.

At first glance, this hotel could be mistaken for a bicycle store or art gallery. Its structure, saved from the original building, contrasts with its interior, which is modern and avant-garde, using a red, white and black color scheme. Details such as the large mural by Hannah Collins in middle of the dining hall, which shows some facades of old businesses in the neighborhood, remind one that the hotel is located right in the old city center.

A simple vista, este hotel podría confundirse con una tienda de bicis o una galería de arte. Su estructura, rescatada del edificio original, contrasta con el interior, de estética moderna y vanguardista, cuya variedad cromática se reduce al rojo, el blanco y el negro. En los pasillos y puertas destaca la personal señalética diseñada en exclusiva para el hotel. Detalles como el gran mural de Hannah Collins en medio del comedor, que muestra algunas fachadas de comercios antiguos del barrio, recuerdan que el hotel se encuentra en pleno centro histórico de la ciudad.

A première vue, cet hôtel pourrait passer pour un magasin de vélos ou une galerie d'art. Sa structure, conservée du bâtiment originel, contraste avec l'intérieur à l'esthétique moderne et avant-garde dont la variété chromatique se réduit au rouge, au blanc et au noir. Dans les couloirs et sur les portes se distingue la signalétique personnalisée conçue spécialement pour l'hôtel. Des détails comme la grande fresque de Hannah Collins, au milieu de la salle à manger, représentant des façades de vieilles boutiques du quartier, nous rappellent que l'hôtel se trouve en plein centre historique de la ville.

A prima vista, questo hotel potrebbe essere scambiato per un negozio di biciclette o per una galleria d'arte. È stata mantenuta la struttura dell'edificio originale, che si pone in contrasto con l'interno, di estetica moderna e avveniristica, e con una varietà cromatica limitata al rosso, al bianco e al nero. Nei corridoi e sulle porte spicca la particolare segnaletica disegnata esclusivamente per l'hotel. Alcuni dettagli, come il grande murale di Hannah Collins al centro della zona pranzo che mostra le facciate di antichi negozi del quartiere, ricordano che l'hotel si trova immerso nel centro storico della città.

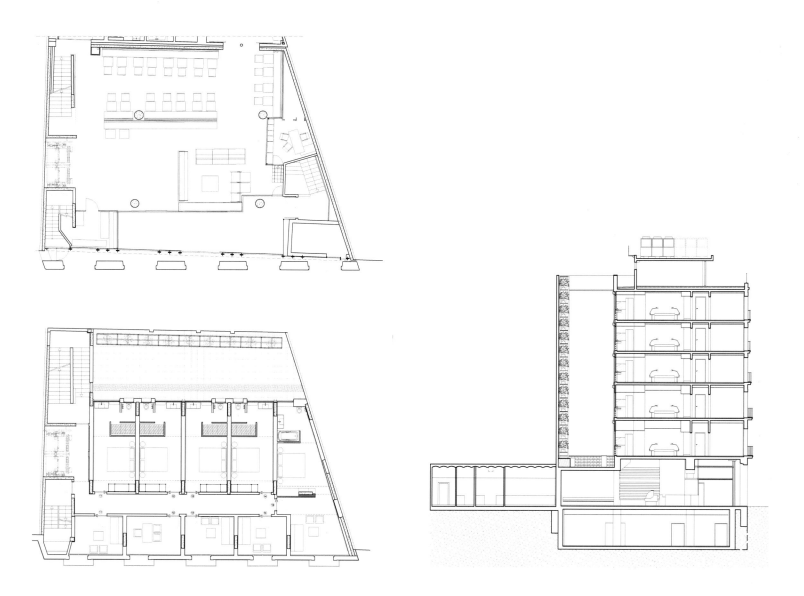

157

Josep Llinàs
Jaume Fuster Library | 2006
Plaça Lesseps 20-22, 08023

Bei der Gestaltung dieses mächtigen und strahlenden Gebäudes ging man von zwei grundlegenden Überlegungen aus. Zunächst muss-te der Hintergrund verstanden werden, den die benachbarten Gebäude bilden, und anschließend die Formen der Bibliothek mit diesem verbunden werden. Dies erreichte man durch einen Grundriss, der von einer rhomboiden Geometrie begrenzt wird, die die Form voll-endet, die von den anderen Gebäuden begonnen wurde. Der zweite Aspekt war die Tatsache, dass sich das Gebäude auf der Grenzli-nie zwischen der Stadt und dem Gebirge und dem übrigen Barcelona befindet. Auch dies wurde in den Baukörpern berücksichtigt, deren Formen und Dach an ein Gebirge erinnern.

The design of this imposing and luminous project stems from two basic considerations. The first is to understand the backdrop pro-vided by the buildings behind it, and blend the library's volume with them. This aim is reflected on the ground floor where its bound-aries are limited by a rhomboidal geometry that completes the volume initiated by the other buildings. The second is that the building is located near the city-mountain limit that separates it from the rest of Barcelona, something which is reflected in its volumes, which emulate these mountain attributes in shape, particularly its roof.

El diseño de este imponente y luminoso proyecto nace de dos consideraciones básicas. La primera, entender el telón de fondo que conforman los edificios posteriores y fundir el volumen de la biblioteca con ellos. Este objetivo queda reflejado en la planta al definir su límite con una geometría romboidal que completa el volumen iniciado por las otras edificaciones. La segunda, que el edificio se encuentra en el límite de la ciudad-montaña y el resto de Barcelona, algo que queda reflejado en sus volúmenes, que emulan estos atributos montañosos en las formas y la cubierta.

La conception de ce projet imposant et lumineux est née de deux considérations de départ. Tout d'abord, comprendre la toile de fond constituée par les bâtiments existants pour y fondre le volume de la bibliothèque. Ce premier objectif est illustré par la forme en tra-pèze de la base qui vient ainsi compléter le volume des autres bâtiments. Ensuite, sa situation à la limite de la ville-montagne et du reste de Barcelone que l'on retrouve dans sa conception. Les caractéristiques de la montagne sont reprises dans ses formes et dans son toit.

Il disegno di questo imponente e luminoso progetto nasce da due considerazioni di base: la prima, comprendere lo sfondo conformato dagli edifici retrostanti e fondervi il volume della biblioteca. Questo obiettivo si riflette nella pianta, i cui limiti sono definiti da una geome-tria romboidale che completa la volumetria originata dalle altre costruzioni. La seconda, che l'edificio si trova al confine tra città-monta-gna e il resto di Barcellona, un fattore riflesso nei suoi volumi, che ricordano gli attributi delle montagne per le forme e per la copertura.

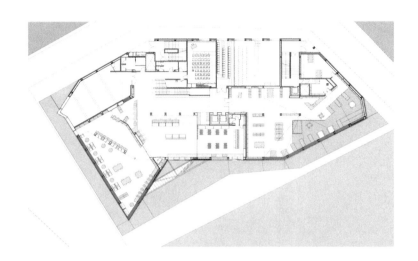

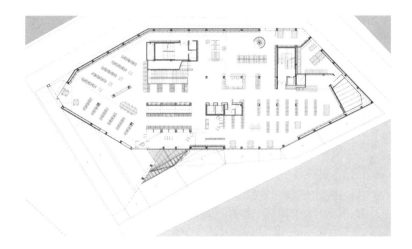

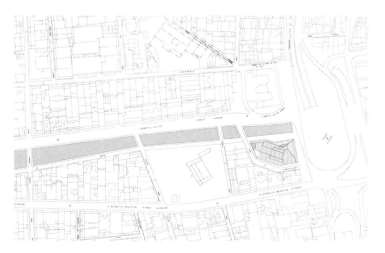

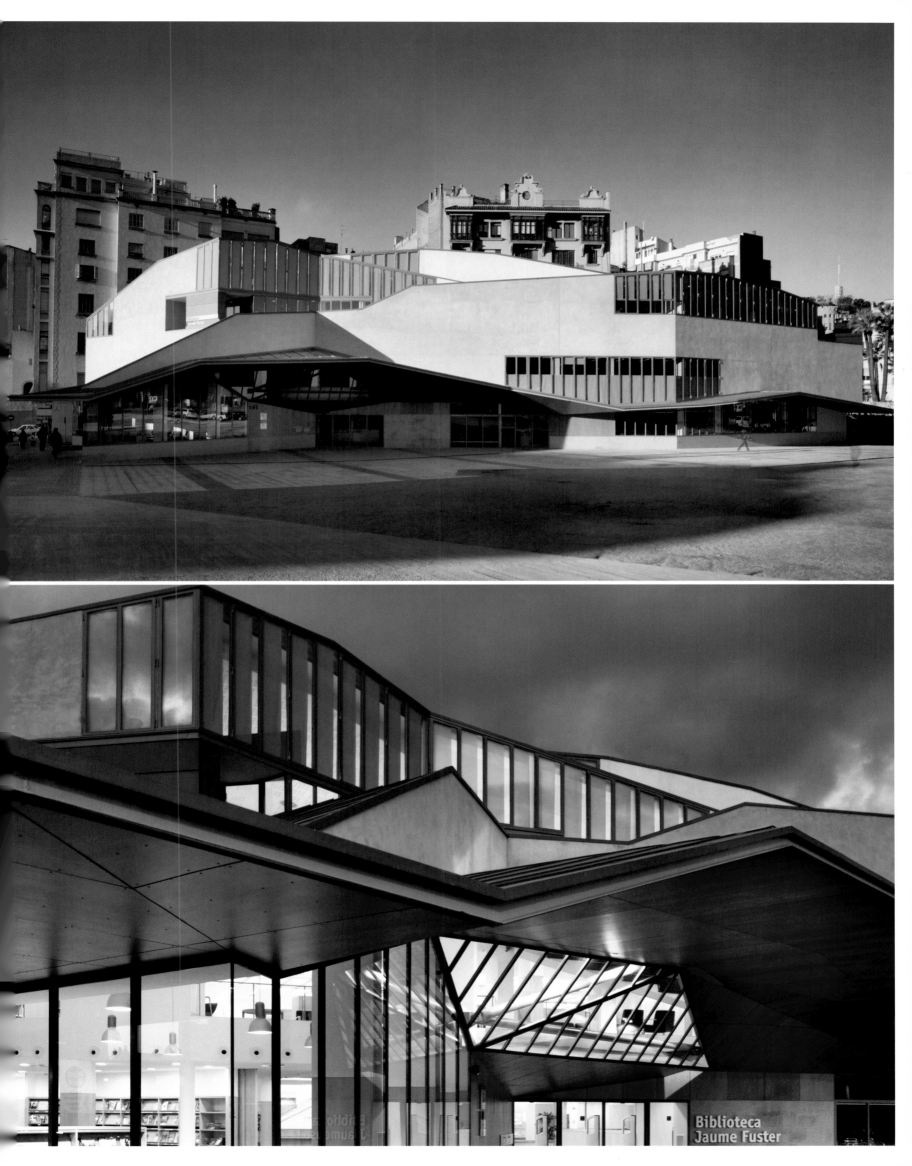

Manuel Ruisánchez Arquitectes

62 Rental Units Apartment Building ⎮ 2006
Travessera de les Corts 86-94, 08028

Dieses Gebäude wurde im Rahmen der Sanierung des Stadtviertels umgestaltet, in dem es sich befindet, nämlich des Viertels Les Corts. Außer Mietwohnungen für junge Menschen beherbergt das Gebäude im Erdgeschoss einen Kindergarten mit Innenhof und soziale Einrichtungen. In den beiden hohen Strukturen, eine mit vier und eine mit sieben Stockwerken, liegen die 38 m² großen Wohnungen mit offenem Grundriss. Bei der Planung war das Einsparen von Energie einer der grundlegenden Aspekte.

This project forms part of a plan for renovating the area where it's located: the Les Corts neighborhood. In addition to homes for young people, the building includes lower levels with a day-care center with an interior patio and outbuildings for social services. On the two raised structures, of four and seven floors, we find homes that were projected to be 125 sq ft of open space. Saving energy resources was an essential part of this project's design.

El proyecto forma parte de un plan de renovación de la zona donde se encuentra: el barrio de Les Corts. Además de las viviendas de alquiler para jóvenes, el edificio incluye en los niveles inferiores una guardería con patio interior y dependencias para los servicios sociales. En las dos estructuras que se alzan, de cuatro y siete pisos, se encuentran las viviendas proyectadas como espacios abiertos de 38 m². El ahorro en usos energéticos ha sido una premisa esencial en el diseño del proyecto.

Le projet fait partie du plan de rénovation de la zone où il se trouve : le quartier de Les Corts. Outre les appartements à louer destinés aux jeunes, on trouve dans les niveaux inférieurs : une garderie avec une cour intérieure et des dépendances pour les services sociaux. Les deux structures, de quatre et sept étages, accueillent les appartements pensés comme des espaces ouverts de 38 m². L'économie d'énergie a constitué l'un des points essentiels dans l'élaboration du projet.

Il progetto è inquadrato nel contesto di un piano di rinnovamento della zona in cui si colloca: il quartiere di Les Corts. Oltre alle abitazioni in affitto destinate ai più giovani, l'edificio accoglie ai livelli inferiori un asilo con cortile interno e locali per i servizi sociali. Nelle due strutture superiori, di quattro e sette livelli rispettivamente, si trovano le residenze progettate come spazi aperti di 38 metri quadrati. Il risparmio degli usi energetici è stata una premessa essenziale dell'elaborazione del progetto.

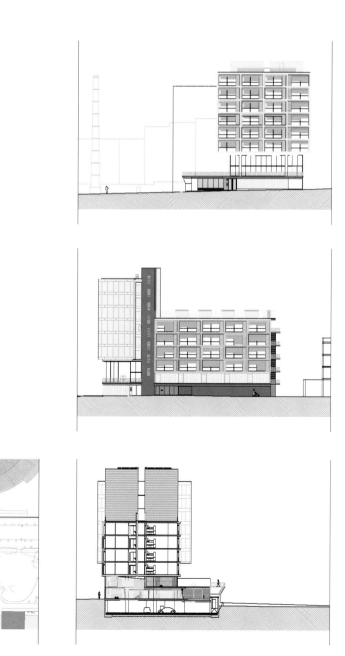

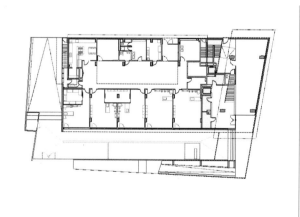

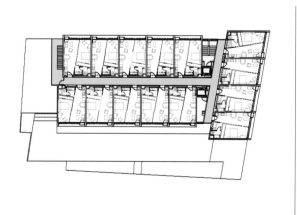

MAP Architects / Josep Lluís Mateo

C.Z.F. Offices | 2005

Taulat s/n, 08019

Der obere Teil dieses majestätischen Gebäudes erhebt sich über einer Basis und wirkt fast wie aufgehängt. Er ist mit einer doppelten Schicht Glas verkleidet. Nachts wirkt die Struktur wie ein Leuchtturm, der die Stadt an seine Präsenz erinnert. Kleine farbige Lichter erklimmen die Fassade des Gebäudes, dessen Form sich in verschiedene Teile auflöst, die in ihrer Gestalt und ihrer Struktur von dem massiven, unverputztem Betonkern vereinheitlicht werden.

The upper part of this majestic building, which is constructed over the foundation as if hanging from it, has been covered with a double glass layer. At night the structure looks as if it were a lighthouse, which reminds the city as to its presence. Small colored lights climb up the building's façade, with a volume that breaks down into various pieces that are formally and structurally joined by its solid concrete nucleus.

La parte superior de este majestuoso edificio, que se alza sobre la base casi como colgando de ella, está revestida de doble capa de vidrio. De noche, esta estructura se observa como si de un faro se tratara, que recuerda y muestra a la ciudad su presencia. Pequeñas luces de colores trepan por la fachada del edificio, cuyo volumen se descompone en piezas diversas unificadas formal y estructuralmente por el macizo núcleo de hormigón aparente.

La partie supérieure de ce majestueux bâtiment reposant sur sa base comme s'il y était suspendu, est recouverte d'une double couche de verre. La nuit, cette structure ressemble à un phare et rappelle sa présence à la ville. De petites lumières de couleurs montent le long de la façade dont le volume se décompose en différents éléments unifiés formellement et structurellement par le noyau de béton massif apparent.

La parte superiore di questo maestoso edificio si stacca dalla base, che dà l'impressione di essere appesa al suo volume, ed è rivestita con una doppia pelle di vetro. Di sera, la struttura assume l'aspetto di un faro, che ricorda e mostra alla città la sua presenza. Piccole luci colorate si arrampicano lungo la facciata dell'edificio, il cui volume si scompone in parti diverse unificate sia a livello formale che strutturale dal visibilissimo nucleo massiccio di calcestruzzo.

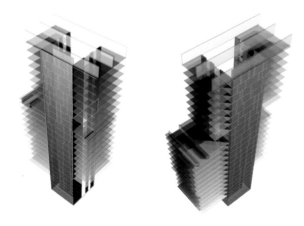

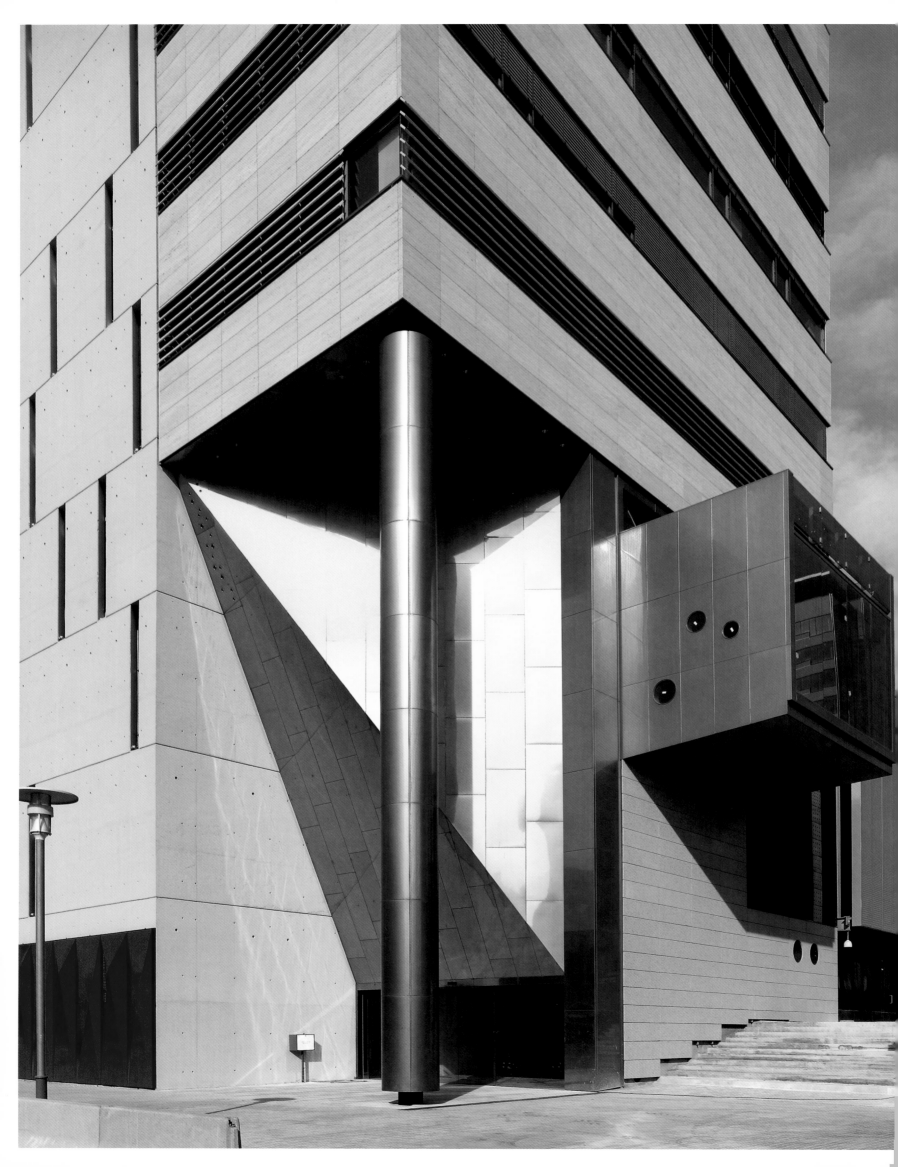

MAP Architects/Josep Lluís Mateo

Hotel AC Barcelona | 2004
Taulat s/n, 08019

Das Hotel AC Barcelona liegt in dem neuen Geschäftsviertel gegenüber dem Forum. Es erhebt sich über einem würfelförmigen Eingang, zu dem man in den anliegenden, hohen und langen Bau gelangt. Das Erscheinungsbild wirkt mit seiner kristallartigen Geometrie und den Steinverkleidungen eher hart. Die Höhe wird durch einen großen, waagerechten Einschnitt unterteilt. An der Fassade dominieren grauer Beton und die Farbe Rot. Das Raster der Fenster ist auf der ganzen Seite sichtbar. Das typische Erscheinungsbild dieser Hotelkette ist im Inneren zu finden, das von weiten Räumen, edlen Materialien und einer gepflegten Dekoration gekennzeichnet ist.

The Hotel AC Barcelona is located in the city's new business center, in front of the Forum. This building was built over a cubic entrance that gives onto the adjacent construction, which is tall and slim. The overall appearance is hard, with crystalline geometry and a rocky finish, and a large horizontal gash that divides its height. Gray concrete and the color red predominate on its façade, which displays square windows along the whole side. We can find the chain's stamp in its interior, which prioritizes spaciousness and the meticulous use of noble materials in its décor.

El Hotel AC Barcelona se encuentra en la nueva área empresarial de la ciudad, frente al Fórum. Este edificio se alza en una entrada cúbica que da paso a la construcción anexa, alta y espigada. La apariencia general es dura, de geometría cristalina y acabado pétreo, con un gran corte horizontal que divide su altura. El gris del hormigón y el color rojo predominan en la fachada, que muestra la retícula de ventanas por todo el lateral. El sello de la cadena se deja intuir en el interior, donde impera la amplitud de espacios y el uso de materiales nobles con una cuidada decoración.

L'Hôtel AC Barcelona se trouve dans la nouvelle zone d'affaires de la ville, face au Forum. Ce bâtiment s'élève sur une entrée cubique permettant l'accès à la construction annexe, haute et élancée. L'apparence générale suggère la dureté, avec une géométrie cristalline et une finition en pierre. Une grande coupure horizontale divise le bâtiment. Le gris du béton et le rouge sont prédominants sur la façade, laquelle présente des rangées de fenêtres sur tout le côté. La spécificité de la chaîne s'apprécie à l'intérieur où dominent des espaces amples et des matériaux nobles dans un décor soigné.

L'Hotel AC Barcelona si colloca nel nuovo quartiere affaristico della città, di fronte al Forum. L'edificio si innalza a partire da un'entrata cubica da cui si accede alla costruzione annessa, alta e slanciata. L'aspetto generale è duro, con una geometria cristallina, rifiniture pietrose e un grande taglio orizzontale che lo divide in altezza. Il grigio del calcestruzzo e il rosso predominano sulla facciata, mentre la parte laterale è segnata dalla griglia delle finestre. All'interno si fa notare lo stile della catena, con spazi ampi, materiali nobili e un'attenta decorazione.

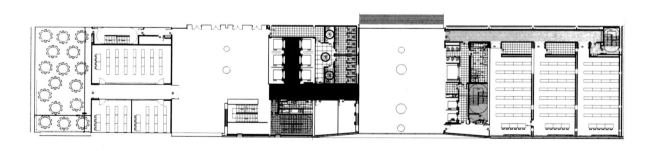

MAP Architects/Josep Lluís Mateo

International Convention Center of Barcelona | 2004
Rambla de Prim 1-17, 08019

Dieses Kongresszentrum wurde anlässlich des Kulturforums 2004 errichtet und besteht aus einer außergewöhnlichen und majestätischen Metallstruktur, die sich am Meer erhebt. Die massive Präsenz und die Kraft der verwendeten Materialien wie Eisen wirken am Standort des Gebäudes nicht unharmonisch, da die metallisierte Fassade die Farbe des Himmels und die Umgebung widerspiegelt. Wo sich die Fassade dem Meer nähert, wirkt sie bewegt und wie eine gewellte, organische Form. Im Inneren liegt ein großer, unterteilbarer Saal neben einem Block, in dem die Diensträume untergebracht sind. Diese Räume öffnen sich zum Meer hin.

This convention center built for the Forum of Cultures 2004, is an enormous and majestic metallic structure that looks out onto the sea. Its striking presence and the strength of a material such as iron don't clash with the area where the building is located, since its metallic facade reflects the color of the sky and its surroundings. On the side closest to the sea, the façade moves and forms an organic, waving front. Inside there's a large dividable hall, along with a block of bathrooms beside it, open towards the sea.

Este centro de convenciones, construido con motivo del Fórum de las Culturas 2004, se asienta como una descomunal y majestuosa estructura metálica frente al mar. Su contundente presencia y la fuerza de un material como el hierro no desentonan en el lugar donde se emplaza el edificio, pues su fachada metalizada refleja el color del cielo en fusión con el entorno. En su lado más cercano al mar, esta fachada se mueve y forma un frente orgánico y ondulante. En el interior se encuentra una gran sala divisible junto con un bloque de servicios anexo, abierto al mar.

Ce centre de conventions, construit à l'occasion du Forum des Cultures 2004, repose sur une majestueuse structure métallique faisant face à la mer. Sa présence imposante et la puissance d'un matériau comme le fer ne détonnent pas dans le lieu où se trouve le bâtiment. En effet, sa façade métallique reflète la couleur du ciel en fusion avec son environnement. Du côté le plus proche de la mer, la façade semble osciller et compose un front organique et ondulant. A l'intérieur, on trouve une salle divisible avec un bloc de services annexes, ouvert sur la mer.

Questo centro congressi, costruito nel contesto del Forum delle Culture del 2004, si colloca come una gigantesca e maestosa struttura metallica di fronte al mare. La sua impressionante presenza e la forza di un materiale come il ferro non si pongono in contrasto con il luogo in cui è ubicato l'edificio, dato che l'involucro metallizzato riflette il colore del cielo fondendosi nel contesto. Dalla parte più vicina al mare, la facciata si muove e forma un fronte organico e ondulante. L'interno accoglie una grande sala configurabile assieme a un volume annesso, con i servizi, aperto al mare.

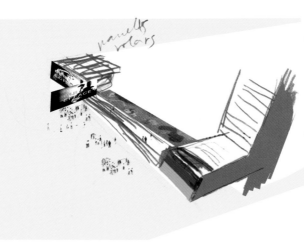

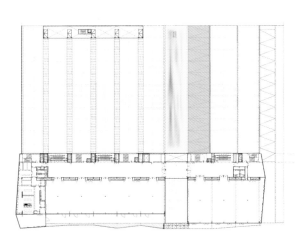

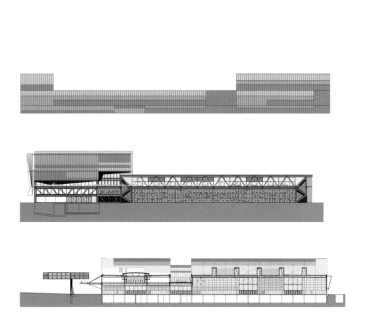

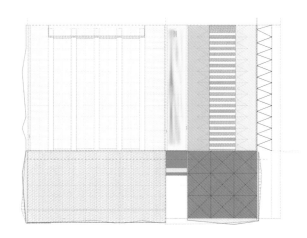

MAP Architects/Josep Lluís Mateo
Sant Jordi Hall of Residence | 2006
Ricardo Zamora 4-8, 08017

Das neue Universitätszentrum Sant Jordi unterteilt sich in drei verschiedene Bereiche, zum einen eine Basis, in der vor allem die gemeinschaftlich genutzten Räume untergebracht sind, dann ein hoher Körper, in dem die meisten Räume liegen und ein weiterer, niedrigerer Körper mit weiteren Räumen und einem Sportplatz. Die Fassade wird von unverputzten Materialien, schwarzen Backsteinen und Zink geprägt. Die farbliche Entwicklung lässt das Gebäude offen und lebendig wirken, so wie ein Universitätszentrum auch wirken sollte. Sie wurde von der Künstlerin Silvia Hornig gestaltet.

The new Sant Jordi Hall of Residence is divided into three different parts: a foundation that essentially contains the elements to be used by the community, a tall body that houses most of the rooms, and a lower body that is made up of some rooms and a sports complex. On the façade we can see materials that reveal its construction, black brick and zinc. The construction's chromatic development gives off the kind of open, vital character that's appropriate of a university center and is the work of artist Silvia Hornig.

El nuevo Colegio Mayor Sant Jordi está dividido en tres partes diferentes: una base que contiene esencialmente los elementos del programa de uso comunitario, el cuerpo alto que alberga la mayoría de las habitaciones y otro cuerpo más bajo que se compone de algunas habitaciones y la pista polideportiva. En la fachada conviven materiales como la obra vista, el ladrillo de color negro o el zinc. El desarrollo cromático de la construcción, que aporta un carácter abierto y vitalista propio de un centro universitario, es obra de la artista Silvia Hornig.

Le nouvelle Résidence Universitaire Sant Jordi est divisée en trois parties: une base qui contient essentiellement les éléments du programme d'utilisation communautaire, la partie la plus élevée accueillant la plupart des chambres et enfin une partie plus basse, composée de quelques chambres et de la piste sportive. La façade est constituée de matériaux tels que le béton apparent, la brique noire ou le zinc. Le déroulement chromatique de la construction, qui apporte un caractère ouvert et vivant adapté à un centre universitaire, est l'oeuvre de l'artiste Silvia Hornig.

Il nuovo Collegio Maggiore Sant Jordi è diviso in tre parti differenti: una base che contiene essenzialmente gli elementi del programma di uso comune, il corpo alto che ospita la maggior parte delle camere e un altro volume più basso che accoglie alcune camere e la pista polisportiva. Nella facciata convivono materiali come il cemento a vista, i mattoni neri e lo zinco. Lo sviluppo cromatico della costruzione, che le attribuisce il carattere aperto e dinamico proprio di un centro universitario, è opera dell'artista Silvia Hornig.

COL·LEGI MAJOR SANT JORDI

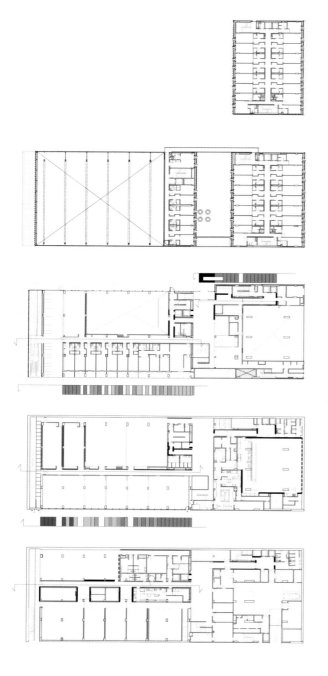

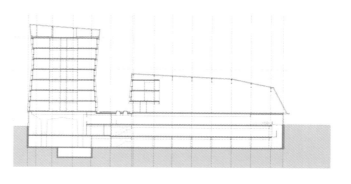

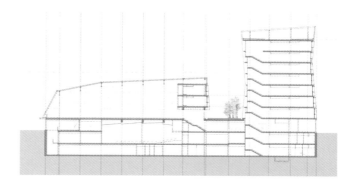

Martínez Lapeña-Torres Arquitectos
Forum Esplanade and Photovoltaic Pergola | 2004
Plaça del Fòrum, 08019

So als ob es sich um ein vom Meer geformtes Delta handeln würde, eine offene Hand mit fünf Fingern, vereint diese Esplanade die Allee Diagonal mit dem Meer. Sie ist wie eine asphaltierte Leinwand mit fünf verschiedenen Farben, ein Patchwork, das mit Höhenunterschieden spielt, Rampen und Freitreppen zum Hafen schafft und eine Steilküste über dem Sporthafen. Auf der anderen Verlängerung der Esplanade befindet sich der Laubengang mit Solarplatten, der die Sonnenenergie in Elektrizität verwandelt und gleichzeitig Schatten spendet.

As if it were a delta by the sea, with the shape of a hand with its five fingers spread wide, this esplanade is located where Diagonal Avenue meets the sea. It's like a canvas of five different colors of asphalt, a *patchwork* that plays with differences in heights, with ramps and steps towards the port area or rocky area around the sports port. On another prolongation of the esplanade we find the photovoltaic pergola, which transforms solar energy into electric energy while also providing shade.

Como si un delta hacia el mar se tratara, con la forma de una mano con los cinco dedos abiertos, esta explanada significa por fin la unión de la avenida Diagonal con el mar. Es como un lienzo de pavimento asfaltado de cinco colores diferentes, un *patchwork* que juega con los desniveles, formando rampas y escalinatas hacia la zona portuaria o acantilados sobre las áreas del puerto deportivo. En otra prolongación de la explanada se encuentra la pérgola fotovoltaica, que transforma la energía solar en eléctrica a la vez que propone un refugio a la sombra.

Semblable à un delta, comme une main ouverte, cette esplanade réalise enfin l'union de la Diagonal et de la mer. Elle suggère une toile en goudron composée de cinq couleurs différentes, un *patchwork* qui joue avec les différences de niveau, formant des rampes et des escaliers vers la zone portuaire ou des falaises surplombant le port de plaisance. Sur un autre prolongement de l'esplanade se trouve la pergola photovoltaïque qui transforme l'énergie solaire en électricité tout en offrant un refuge ombragé.

Come se si trattasse di un delta che sfocia in mare, con la forma di una mano e le cinque dita aperte, la spianata rappresenta finalmente l'unione della Diagonal con il mare. È come una tela di pavimento asfaltato con cinque colori diversi, un patchwork che gioca con i dislivelli, formando rampe e scalinate verso la zona portuale o precipizi sulle aree del porto sportivo. Su uno dei prolungamenti della spianata si colloca la pergola fotovoltaica che trasforma l'energia solare in energia elettrica e allo stesso tempo offre un rifugio all'ombra.

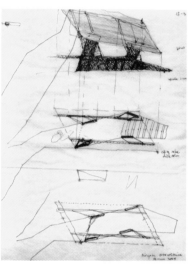

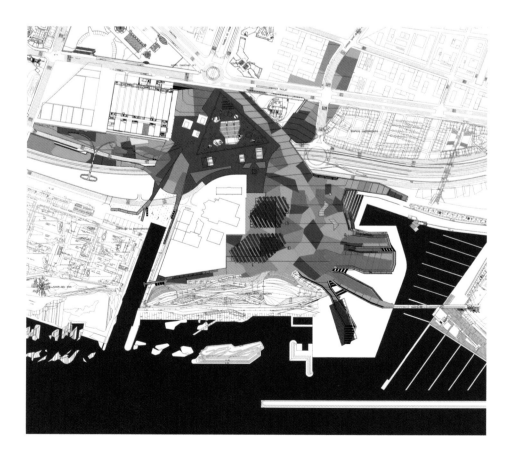

Óscar Tusquets Blanca

AC Gran Hotel Miramar | 2007
Plaça Carlos Ibáñez 3, 08038

Dieses Hotel stellte eine große Herausforderung an die Architekten dar, da an ein bereits existierendes Gebäude aus dem Jahr 1928 eine neue Struktur hinzugefügt werden musste, die die vorhandene jedoch nicht überschatten durfte. Die Fassade des Neubaus ist nach hinten gesetzt, um der alten Fassade die Hauptrolle zu überlassen, und erstreckt sich auf beiden Seiten des Gebäudes. Im Inneren setzte man auf einen modernen Stil mit Stahlelementen und Leder in schlichten Tönen wie Weiß, Braun, Grau und Schwarz in allen Räumen und auch im Garten- und Swimmingpoolbereich.

This project was a great architectural challenge since it was about adding, without eclipsing, a new structure over an existing building which dates back to 1928. The façade of the recent construction stands behind in order to highlight the old façade and extends alongside both sides. Its interior decoration boasts a very modern style, with materials like steel or skins, and sober tones like white, brown, gray and black in all its rooms, as well as in the garden and pool areas.

Este proyecto suponía un gran desafío arquitectónico, pues se trataba de añadir, sin eclipsarla, una nueva estructura al edificio existente, datado de 1928. La fachada de la reciente obra se retranquea hacia atrás para dejar protagonismo al antiguo frente y se extiende adosada a ambos lados. En el interior, la decoración apuesta por un estilo muy moderno, con materiales como el acero o las pieles y en tonos sobrios como blanco, marrones, grises y negros en todas las estancias, así como en la zona de jardín y piscina.

Ce projet représentait un défi architectural majeur. En effet, il s'agissait d'ajouter sans l'éclipser, une nouvelle structure au bâtiment existant, datant de 1928. La façade du nouvel édifice est en retrait pour mieux mettre l'ancienne en valeur, puis elle s'étend des deux côtés du bâtiment. A l'intérieur, la décoration est d'inspiration très moderne, avec des matériaux comme l'acier ou le cuir et des tons sobres comme le blanc, le marron, le gris et le noir que l'on retrouve dans toutes les pièces ainsi que dans la zone du jardin et de la piscine.

Il progetto rappresentava una grande sfida architettonica, dato che prevedeva l'aggiunta di una nuova struttura che non alterasse lo spirito dell'edificio esistente, costruito nel 1928. La nuova facciata si colloca attorno al volume originale e si ritira verso l'interno lasciando in primo piano la struttura preesistente. All'interno, l'arredamento adotta uno stile assai moderno, con materiali come l'acciaio o la pelle in tonalità sobrie come il bianco, il marrone, il grigio e il nero in tutti gli spazi, anche nella zona del giardino e della piscina.

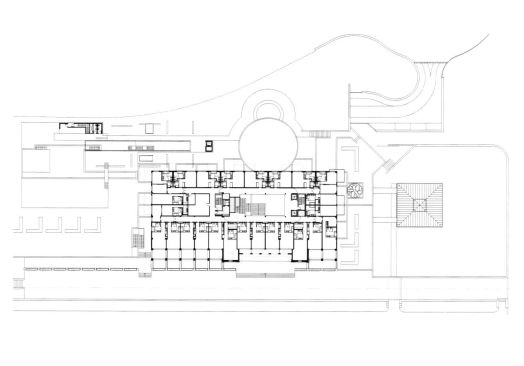

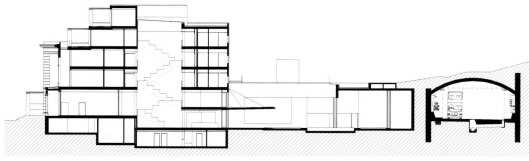

Óscar Tusquets Blanca
Barcelona Princess | 2004
Avinguda Diagonal 1, 08019

Das wichtigste Kennzeichen dieses Hotels ist der seltsame Standort, ein dreieckiges Grundstück, sehr außergewöhnlich für das Viertel Eixample, denn dieses Stadtviertel ist durch seine quadratische Rasterform gekennzeichnet. Die Allee Diagonal durchschneidet dieses Grundstück, auf dem das majestätische Hotel mit seiner blau-orangenen Betonfassade in Kombination mit Aluminium- und Glasplatten errichtet wurde, jedoch. Das Hotel besteht aus drei unabhängigen Strukturen, aus zwei Türmen und einem Laufsteg aus Metall, der sie verbindet. So wurde der vorhandene Platz maximal ausgenutzt.

The main characteristic of this project is its peculiar distribution: a building with a triangular shape, which is especially unique when you consider that it is located in the Eixample neighborhood, which is characterized by its square grid blocks. Nevertheless, Diagonal Avenue divides this block right where they built this majestic hotel with its concrete façade dyed blue and orange, and combined with sheets of glass and aluminum. It consists of three independent structures: two towers and the metal footbridge that connects them, all projected with the intention of maximizing space.

La principal característica de este proyecto es su peculiar emplazamiento: un solar en forma de triángulo, algo excepcional teniendo en cuenta que se encuentra en el barrio del Eixample, caracterizado por su trazado en cuadrículas. No obstante, la avenida Diagonal secciona esta manzana donde se erige majestuoso el hotel, con una fachada de hormigón teñida en azul y naranja combinado con planchas de aluminio y vidrio. Se trata de tres estructuras independientes: las dos torres y la pasarela metálica que las comunica, proyectadas todas con la intención de aprovechar al máximo el espacio.

La singularité principale de ce projet réside dans son emplacement même : un lieu en forme de triangle. C'est assez exceptionnel si l'on pense qu'il se trouve dans le quartier de l'Eixample, caractérisé par ses quadrilataires. Néanmoins, l'avenue Diagonal coupe le pâté de maisons où s'élève ce majestueux hôtel avec sa façade en béton teinté de bleu et d'orange associé à des plaques d'aluminium et de verre. Nous avons ici trois structures différentes : les deux tours et la passerelle métallique qui les unit. Leur conception générale répond à la volonté de mettre à profit tout l'espace disponible.

La caratteristica principale di questo progetto è la sua peculiare ubicazione: un lotto triangolare, un caso eccezionale considerando che si trova nel quartiere dell'Eixample, caratterizzato dal suo schema a griglia. Tuttavia, il corso Diagonal taglia l'isolato in cui si innalza questo maestoso hotel, con un involucro in calcestruzzo azzurro e arancione su cui sono inseriti pannelli di alluminio e vetro. Si tratta di tre strutture indipendenti: le due torri e la passerella metallica che le mette in comunicazione, concepite tutte con l'intenzione di approfittare al massimo lo spazio.

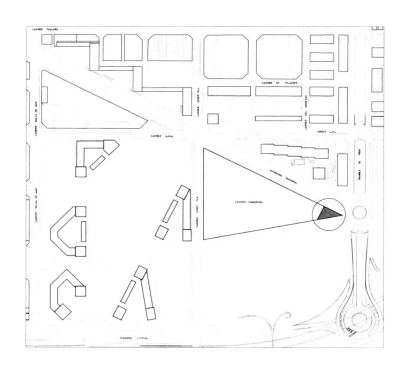

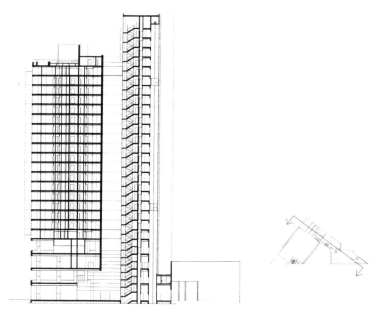

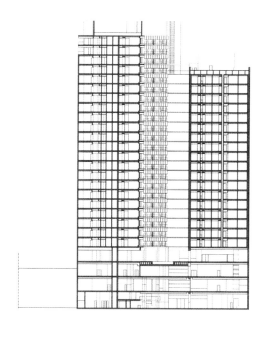

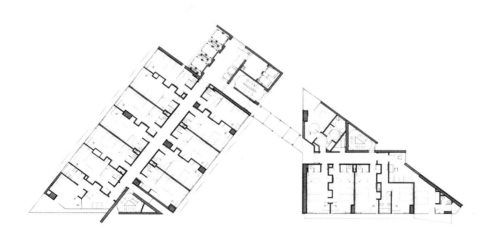

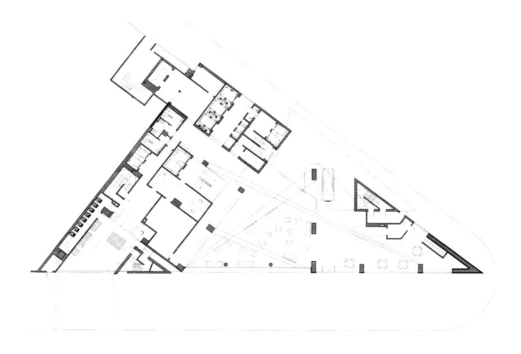

Richard Rogers, Alonso & Balaguer, GCA Arquitectes Associats (interior design)
Hesperia Tower | 2005
Gran Via 144, 08907 L'Hospitalet

Zwei unterschiedliche Bereiche unterteilen diesen Turm. In der niedrigeren Struktur befinden sich die Büroräume, das Kongresszentrum und die Sporteinrichtungen, während in der hohen Struktur die Hotelzimmer liegen, die von der spektakulären, verglasten Kuppel gekrönt werden. Jedes Element wurde innerhalb der architektonischen Gestaltung auf besondere Weise gekennzeichnet. Die Zimmer liegen in dem schwebenden Block, der sich an der Fassade wiederholt. Die Struktur der beiden Ebenen wird von 30 sehr hohen Betonsäulen bestimmt.

Two separate spaces divide this tower. In the lower structure we find the offices, congress center and sports center, while the hotel is located in the tower, which is crowned by a spectacular glass cupola. Each element has been put together in a specific way within the architectural design. The rooms are located inside a floating block repeated on the façade and the structure of the lower levels is conveyed by way of 30, very tall, concrete columns.

Dos espacios diferenciados dividen esta torre. En la estructura de menor altura se encuentran las oficinas, el centro de congresos y el centro deportivo, mientras que la torre acomoda el hotel, coronado por la espectacular cúpula acristalada. Cada elemento ha sido articulado de un modo específico dentro del diseño arquitectónico. Las habitaciones se encuentran dentro de un bloque flotante repetido en la fachada y la estructura en los niveles inferiores se expresa a través de 30 columnas de hormigón de gran altura.

Cette tour se divise en deux espaces différents. La structure la plus basse accueille les bureaux, le centre de conférences et le centre sportif. La tour accueille l'hôtel couronné par une spectaculaire coupole en verre. Chaque élément a trouvé une place spécifique dans le concept architectural de l'ensemble. Les chambres se trouvent dans un bloc flottant se répétant le long de la façade et la structure des niveaux inférieurs comporte 30 colonnes en béton de grande hauteur.

Due spazi differenziati dividono questa torre. La struttura di minor altezza accoglie gli uffici, il centro congressi e il centro sportivo, mentre la torre ospita l'hotel, coronato dalla spettacolare cupola vetrata. Ogni elemento è stato articolato in modo specifico all'interno del progetto architettonico. Le camere si trovano all'interno di un volume aggettante ripetuto sulla facciata opposta, mentre la struttura dei livelli inferiori è composta da 30 colonne di calcestruzzo di grande altezza.

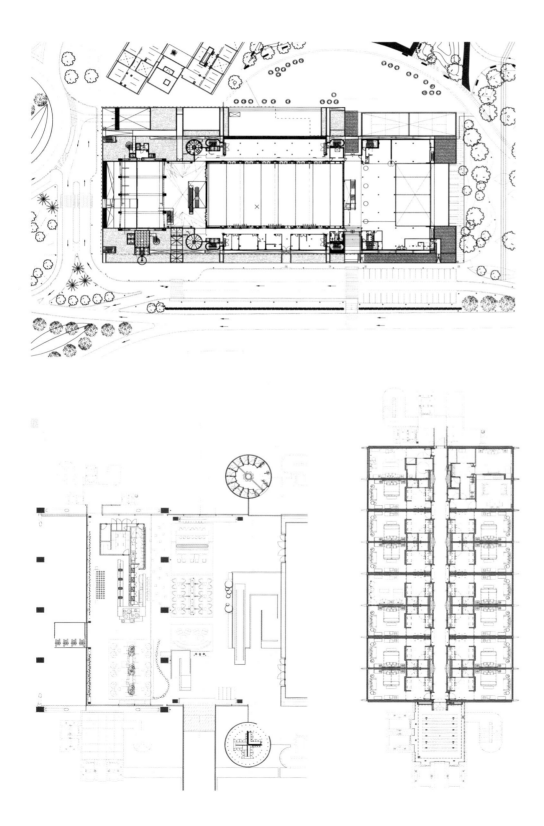

ADD+Arquitectura/Xavier Claramunt
Palo Alto. Pellaires 30-38, Nau G01
08019 Barcelona, Spain
P +34 933 034 660
F +34 933 034 665
add.arquitectura@coac.net
www.xclaramunt.com
Hotel Chic & Basic Born
Photos © Rafael Vargas

Ateliers Jean Nouvel
10, Cité d'Angoulême
75011 Paris, France
P +33 1 49 23 83 83
F +33 1 43 14 81 10
info@jeannouvel.fr
www.jeannouvel.com
Agbar Tower
Photos © Òscar Garcia

b720 Arquitectos
Josep Tarradelles 123
08029 Barcelona, Spain
P +34 933 637 979
F +34 933 630 139
fermin.vazquez@b720.com
www.b720.com
Agbar Tower
Photos © Òscar Garcia
Indra Offices
Photos © Rafael Vargas

BAAS/Jordi Badia
Montserrat de Casanovas 105
08032 Barcelona, Spain
P +34 933 580 111
baas@jordibadia.com
www.jordibadia.com
Refurbishment of a Commercial Space into an Office
Photos © Eugeni Pons

Brullet-Pineda Arquitectes
Travessera de Dalt 93
08024 Barcelona, Spain
P +34 932 106 825
F +34 932 100 214
pinearq@pinearq.com
www.pinearq.com
Barcelona Biomedical Research Park
Photos © Jordi Miralles

Capella García Arquitectura
Casp 108, 7è
08010 Barcelona, Spain
P +34 932 651 369
F +34 932 460 949
info@capellaweb.com
www.capellaweb.com
Hotel Diagonal Barcelona
Photos © Rafael Vargas

Carlos Ferrater
Balmes 145, baixos
08008 Barcelona, Spain
P +34 932 385 136
carlos@ferrater.com
www.ferrater.com
Botanical Institute of Barcelona
Photos © Alejo Bagué
Social Services of Fort Pienc Neighborhood
Photos © Alejo Bagué

CCT Arquitectos
Puerto Príncipe 26-40, 1er 12è
08027 Barcelona, Spain
P +34 934 080 367
F +34 934 082 539
cct@coac.es
www.cctarquitectos.com
Julie Sohn Boutique
Photos © Eugeni Pons

Clotet, Paricio i Associats/Lluís Clotet, Ignasi Paricio
Pujades 63, 3 principal
08005 Barcelona, Spain
P +34 934 853 625
F +34 933 090 567
cpa@coac.net
Illa de la Llum
Photos © Lluís Casals

EMBT/Enric Miralles-Benedetta Tagliabue
Passatge de la Pau 10 bis, principal
08002 Barcelona, Spain
P +34 934 125 342
F +34 934 123 718
www.mirallestagliabue.com
Gas Natural Headquarters
Photos © Jordi Miralles
Restoration of Santa Caterina Market
Photos © Duccio Malagamba

Futur-2
Roc Boronat 37
08005 Barcelona, Spain
P +34 934 853 100
F +34 934 864 049
info@futur-2.com
www.futur-2.com
Sugar Club
Photos © Marc Llibre Roig

GCA Arquitectes Associats
València 289
08009 Barcelona, Spain
P + 34 934 761 800
F + 34 934 761 806
info@gcaarq.com
www.gcaarq.com
Evo Restaurant
Photos © Jordi Miralles
Olivia Plaza Hotel
Photos © Jordi Miralles
Oriol Balaguer's Cake Shop
Photos © Jordi Miralles
QK Boutique
Photos © Jordi Miralles

Herzog & de Meuron
Rheinschanze 6
4056 Basel, Switzerland
P + 41 61 385 57 57
F + 41 61 385 57 58
Forum Building
Photos © Duccio Malagamba

Jaime Hayón
Muntaner 88, 2on 1a
08011 Barcelona, Spain
P + 34 935 321 776
info@hayonstudio.com
www.hayonstudio.com
Camper Store
Photos © Camper

Jordi Tió, Ferran Amat (interior design)
bcn@vincon.com
tio@coac.es
Hotel Casa Camper
Photos © Camper

Josep Llinàs
Avinguda República Argentina 74, entresòl
08023 Barcelona, Spain
P + 34 932 131 098
F + 34 932 855 369
llinas@coac.net
Jaume Fuster Library
Photos © Julio Cunill

Manuel Ruisánchez Arquitectes, S.L.
Aribau 282, 6è 5ena
08006, Barcelona, Spain
P + 34 934 141 614
F + 34 934 144 333
arq@ruisanchez.net
www.ruisanchez.net
62 Rental Units Apartment Building
Photos © Teresa Llodrés

MAP Architects / Josep Lluís Mateo
Teodoro Roviralta 39
08022 Barcelona, Spain
P + 34 932 186 358
F + 34 932 185 292
map@mateo-maparchitect.com
www.mateo-maparchitect.com
C.Z.F. Offices
Photos © Duccio Malagamba
Hotel AC Barcelona
Photos © Jordi Miralles
International Convention Center of Barcelona
Photos © Infinite Light, Beat Marugg
Sant Jordi Hall of Residence
Photos © Beat Marugg

Martínez Lapeña-Torres Arquitectos
Roca i Batlle 14, 1er
08023 Barcelona, Spain
jamlet@arquired.es
Forum Esplanade and Photovoltaic Pergola
Photos © Martínez Lapeña-Torres Arquitectos

Óscar Tusquets Blanca
Cavallers 50
08034 Barcelona, Spain
P + 34 932 065 580
F + 34 932 804 071
info@tusquets.com
www.tusquets.com
AC Gran Hotel Miramar
Photos © Jordi Miralles
Barcelona Princess
Photos © Gunnar Knetchel, Rafael Vargas

Richard Rogers
(in colaboration with Alonso & Balaguer and
GCA Arquitectes Associats)
Thames Wharf
Rainville Road
W6 9HA London, United Kingdom
P + 44 20 73 85 12 35
F + 44 20 73 85 84 09
enquiries@rsh-p.com
www.richardrogers.co.uk
Hesperia Tower
Photos © Gogortza & Llorella / Bisoufoto

© 2007 daab
cologne london new york

published and distributed worldwide by
daab gmbh
friesenstr. 50
d - 50670 köln

p + 49 - 221 - 913 927 0
f + 49 - 221 - 913 927 20

mail@daab-online.com
www.daab-online.com

publisher ralf daab
rdaab@daab-online.com

creative director feyyaz
mail@feyyaz.com
DAS F - PRINZIP® © 2007 feyyaz

editorial project by loft publications
© 2007 loft publications

editor and text aitana lleonart

layout ignasi gracia blanco
english translation antonio moreno
french translation eulogio barrio
italian translation quirino di zitti
german translation susanne engler

front and back cover © jordi miralles

printed in czech republic
www.graspo.com

isbn 978-3-86654-029-3